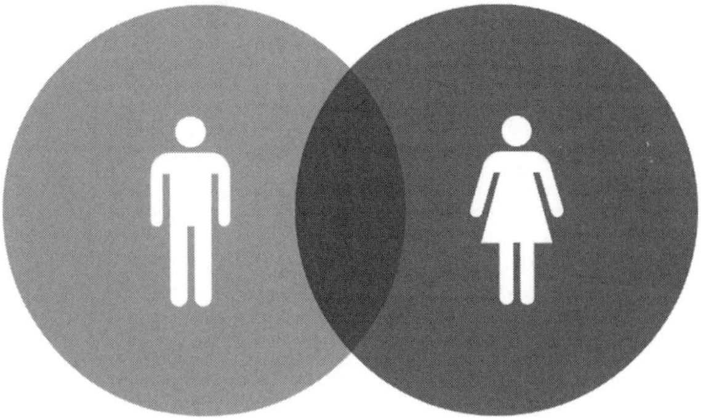

TRANSGENDER 101

A SIMPLE GUIDE TO A COMPLEX ISSUE

NICHOLAS M. TEICH, LCSW

FOREWORD BY JAMISON GREEN

COLUMBIA UNIVERSITY PRESS

NEW YORK

COLUMBIA UNIVERSITY PRESS
Publishers Since 1893
New York Chichester, West Sussex

Library of Congress Cataloging-in-Publication Data
Teich, Nicholas M.
Transgender 101: a simple guide to a complex issue / Nicholas M. Teich;
foreword by Jamison Green.
p. cm.
Includes bibliographical references and index.
ISBN 978-0-231-15712-4 (cloth : alk. paper) — ISBN 978-0-231-15713-1
(pbk. : alk. paper) 1. Transgenderism. 2. Transgender
people. 3. Transsexuals. I. Title.
HQ77.9.T45 2011
306.76'8—dc23 2011025623

Casebound editions of Columbia University Press books are printed
on permanent and durable acid-free paper.

Printed in the United States of America
c 10 9 8 7 6 5 4 3 2 1

This book is dedicated to my parents, Susan and Robert Teich.
Their support and encouragement are awe inspiring.

CONTENTS

FOREWORD

Jamison Green

Many transgender people tell their stories, or use their own feelings and descriptions of their connections to others as a vehicle through which to "normalize" their experience, to make an idea of "trans-ness" comprehensible to people who have no idea what it might feel like. Those who experience their gender as different from their sex are constantly aware of that difference—even if the difference is not visible to others—and they often search for ways to explain their experience. Writers have always tried to work their verbal magic by creating emotional reactions in their readers; and in the case of transpeople, the primary emotion most writers seek to evoke is empathy—the sense of shared experience. This book is not that kind of book. This book is an invocation to empathy through reason, not emotion.

Nick Teich explains what it means to be transgender in a refreshingly clear way. His text is aimed at a wide audience, including young adults seeking to contextualize concepts they have read about in the press or in theoretical settings and anyone who's had some limited exposure to transpeople and who wants to learn more without prying deeply into a single individual's personal life events. Autobiographical accounts can be uncomfortably awkward, marred by authors' assumptions that their experiences and observations matter, when they haven't properly laid the groundwork to engage their readers' trust. Nick's straightforward approach casts light on the social realities of transpeople in America without unduly burdening the reader with personality particularities. Yet he also manages to convey the humanity of his subject. For example, his chapter on coming out touches succinctly on the dynamics of relationships between transpeople and the various roles we play in other people's lives as children, parents, siblings, spouses or partners, and coworkers, with just enough detail to make readers aware of the nuances each of us faces.

Nick's perspective is particular to contemporary Western experience, especially when examining the controversy over the path to medical treatment that leads through the territory of mental health. To receive treatment, in most cases, transpeople are tasked with demonstrating to a mental health professional that we are stable, capable people, and that we can understand the ramifications of treatment. After spending our entire lives coming to grips with our gender and reaching a decision on a course of action—particularly for adults—having to ask permission to finally move forward is often perceived as frustrating, if not insulting. Nick presents the controversies and the complexities of this process in a way that invites readers to consider how their own opinions stack up against the prevailing standards, which are guaranteed to change in some way over the next several years with the introduction of the fifth edition of the American Psychiatric Association's *Diagnostic and Statistical Manual of Mental Disorders* (*DSM-5*) and the World Professional Association for Transgender Health's seventh edition of the Standards of Care. The grounding that Nick provides in these issues will help the inquisitive reader contextualize the coming changes.

Nick's chapter on the discrimination that transpeople face on a daily basis is enlightening because it grounds the reader in the cognitive processes and historical presumptions about people that most Americans carry around unconsciously. Nick's ideas throughout the book both inform and offer understanding, as well as setting up plenty of opportunities for deeper exploration for students or the enterprising, inquisitive reader.

Transgender concepts and experience are still mystifying or even offensive to many people, but those who look below the surface to see the human beings affected by gender variance—and the social systems that have led to and exacerbate the condition—cannot help but be moved. With this book, Nick Teich's contribution toward the kind of understanding that is needed to build a world that is safe for transgender people goes far beyond the summer camp for transgender kids that he started in 2009. Yet that camp, as he modestly describes in his introduction, is literally saving the lives of both children and parents. When it comes to making a difference, Nick's inspirational efforts are worthy of commendation.

INTRODUCTION

Why This Book Was Written and How It Is Laid Out

Why write this book?

To paraphrase Renaissance philosopher Sir Francis Bacon, "knowledge is power." Over the past several years, I have spent innumerable hours reading about, discussing, and teaching people on the subject of transgenderism. I have found that even the most educated people know little of the subject, through no fault of their own. I found it disheartening that my professors in social work school, many of them practicing therapists, knew little to nothing about transpeople. I tried to think what I might know about the subject if I wasn't living it. Would I know anything? Some things? A lot? I find these questions difficult to answer, and it doesn't much matter. By writing *Transgender 101*, I have set out to educate people of all stripes about the basics of what it means to be a transgender person. There are many clinical textbooks, first-person accounts, and journal articles on different subjects surrounding transgenderism, but I found that a reasonably short, concise introduction to the topic, aimed at a wide audience, simply did not exist. If this book can help people better understand their transgender brethren, then that is all I can ask for.

WHAT LED ME TO THIS TOPIC

I was labeled female at birth. Though as a young child I constantly told people that I wanted to be a boy and often blended in as one, it wasn't until after college, and after a long struggle with a deep depression, that I let the idea of transitioning from female to male take hold. Although this book is not an autobiography, there are highly personal reasons that led me to sit down and decide that I wanted to publish information about what it means to be transgender.

In 2009, I started the world's first summer camp program dedicated to transgender youth, called Camp Aranu'tiq. It is presently a week-long camp where kids do what kids do at camp: an array of different daytime activities on land and water, campfires, playing capture the flag, singing silly songs, staying up late to talk with bunkmates—you get the picture. It's a place for trans youth to feel safe and normal. There aren't too many places like that for trans kids or adults, unfortunately. I have been a summer camp person all my life. I attended a camp in Maine where I subsequently became a counselor, spending a total of thirteen summers there. I still go back often to visit. I always knew that I was very lucky to be able to go to camp. Though I may have presented as a boy, I was known as a girl. At camp my gender seemed to melt away; I was just able to be me.

After I entered the adult world and stopped going to camp for the full summer, I started spending one week in August volunteering at a charity-based summer camp. I loved doing it and became close with staff members who returned year after year. When I announced my impending gender transition to the staff of this camp, I was initially met with enthusiastic support, and I was relieved that my relationship would stay intact. However, in a complete change of attitude, months later the camp's director told me that I could not return "for the good of the kids." I was also told that the campers' parents would likely be upset if

I continued to volunteer there because, I was told, "a lot of them probably watch *Jerry Springer*" (and thus would think that I belonged on that show and not at camp). After that, most everyone involved with the camp ceased to have contact with me. Though emotionally that loss was one of the most difficult I endured during my transition, it forced me to think. I thought not only about trans adults who are discriminated against, but children as well. What happens to kids who realize their transgender identity at a young age? What camp could they possibly attend? Certainly not a single-sex camp. But even at coed camps, the kids are split up into groups of "boys" and "girls." What about someone who was assigned one sex at birth but identifies as another? What about kids who don't know how they identify but know that they are not "boys" or "girls"?

Seventeen months after these thoughts finally solidified in my head, Camp Aranu'tiq had its first summer week, with forty-one campers and over twenty volunteer staff. The incredible positive transformation of everyone involved was, and still is, beyond words for me. I am so proud of the campers for having the courage to be themselves and the staff for taking a chance and subsequently changing lives. It is my hope that in my lifetime I will see all summer camps accept transgender youth just like any other camper.

For one year during my master's program in clinical social work, I spent three days a week as an intern doing psychotherapy with young adults, a few of whom were transgender. The insight I gained during that time was very valuable. The journey is different for every person in every way, including the timeline, the events leading up to the realization of being transgender, the support systems (or lack thereof), and the struggle with depression, anxiety, and sometimes even suicide.

I learned from this therapy as well as from personal experiences and those of close friends that the tough stuff transpeople endure is almost always due to the stigma that comes with being transgender. The depression, the anxiety, the thought that life is not worth living—this often comes from thoughts transpeople have that they are freaks, sick, perverted, ungodly, and crazy. "And," a transperson might think, "even if I were able to get over all of this, what would my family and friends say? I could not dream of doing this to them." Loss of job, status, and respect are concerns that swirl around in transpeople's heads. All of these thoughts are creations of our human society. They don't exist in the rest of the animal kingdom.

A FEW WORDS OF ADVICE

Some transgender people readily answer nearly every question that people ask about being transgender, including questions that no one would ever dream of asking a nontransperson (namely, anatomy-related questions). When transpeople reveal their trans identity to someone, it is a highly personal moment. It takes trust and courage to talk about gender identity or gender transition. If the transperson invites a no-holds-barred question-and-answer session, then ask whatever you wish. But most people draw a fine line between what is someone else's business and what is not. That being said, it is very difficult to be able to say, "I don't feel comfortable sharing that." Most people are unaccustomed to being told that something is not their business, at least not in everyday conversation. The person who asked the question may be overly apologetic, and then both parties end up feeling embarrassed. This is not necessary. It is important to be respectful. The best case scenario is probably to: (1) ask what, if any, questions are appropriate; and (2) to give the transperson an out if he or she feels like you are overstepping your bounds (even though your questions may be born of an innocent curiosity). This makes it easier for a transperson to maintain privacy and integrity.

A MAP OF THIS BOOK

Chapter 1, "What Does It Mean to Be Transgender?" focuses on answering that question in as simple yet as concrete a way as possible. It begins by calling into question your view of your own gender. We will move through some important definitions such as sex, gender identity, gender expression, and the gender binary. Some examples and helpful tables will lead you through this material. Chapter 1 discusses how to refer to different transpeople as well as the estimates of the numbers of transpeople that exist today.

Chapter 2, "Sexual Orientation Versus Gender," looks at the differences and similarities between the words *straight, gay, lesbian, bisexual*, and *transgender*. We will define some more terms and look at scales and spectra that are used informally to measure sexual orientation and different aspects of gender. We will go over what might be confusing about differentiating between sexual orientation and gender and why the two are often conflated. Chapter 2 covers marriage and relationship legality issues due to gender and sexual orientation as well as a bit about the communities of gay, lesbian, and bisexual versus transgender and why they do not always get along.

Chapter 3, "Coming Out as Transgender," discusses the ways in which transpeople come out, or reveal their trans identities, and the ways in which they do not. It explores the common reactions from different people when a transperson comes out (e.g., family, friends, others) and outlines the steps that some people go through to try to accept someone's trans identity. Chapter 3 also touches on transgender children and their coming out.

Chapter 4, "Transition," outlines the multifaceted transition process that many transgender people go through. This includes social transition, changing documentation, surgeries, hormone regimens, and an explanation about how some transgender people do not go through any medical transition (surgery and/or hormones). Chapter 4 also includes a brief description of transgender kids and what some of their transition processes might look like.

Chapter 5, "The History of Transgenderism and Its Evolution Over Time," looks at some historical figures in the trans movement, a timeline of trans events in America, and a little bit of biology and evolution that might lead us to think about transgenderism as something that is completely natural. We will also briefly explore transgenderism in other cultures, both in history and today. We will look at one famous case example, that of David Reimer, who endured a botched circumcision and was subsequently raised female until his teenage years, and how this case impacted the nature versus nurture debate.

Chapter 6, "Transgenderism as a Mental Health Issue," discusses the controversy surrounding gender identity disorder and why some transgender people continue to be diagnosed with it. We will look at some examples and different sides of the ongoing debate, as well as the changes that are currently being made to the diagnosis.

Chapter 7, "Discrimination," explores some different ways that people, both consciously and unconsciously, discriminate against transgender people. We will look at nondiscrimination and hate crime laws, the debate over public restroom use for transgender people, custody issues, a study that shows what transgender kids face in schools, discrimination in religion and the military, and what it means to pass as a nontransgender person.

Chapter 8, "Lesser-Known Types of Transgenderism," shows us different kinds of gender identity and expression that are found under the umbrella of transgenderism but that are often left out altogether. These include drag queens, genderqueer people, two-spirit people, cross-dressers, and gender-variant and gender-nonconforming people. We will also look at the difference between transgender people and those with disorders of sex development (sometimes known as intersex) and how these two are not mutually exclusive terms. The chapter ends with a reflection on what we have discussed in the book and what one might do with this information.

A glossary of terms and resources for readers are given at the end of the book. When reading the glossary, keep in mind that there are many more terms than I have listed there that transgender and nontranspeople alike use to describe gender-related phenomena. I believe that language often boxes people in instead of freeing them to be who they are. However, as human beings, we communicate using language as part of our daily existence, so it is important to define some terms. Most of the terms in the glossary are ones I use within the chapters of this book. Other people may use variations of these definitions and, likewise, the definitions of these terms may evolve over time.

A NOTE BEFORE WE GET STARTED

My hope is that you who read this book will enjoy yourselves and gain enough insight to be able to tell others that transgenderism is not about what people see on shows like *Jerry Springer*. It's about people trying to find their way through life just like anyone else. It's about people being themselves and hoping to be content with who they really are. Isn't that all any of us can ask for?

ACKNOWLEDGMENTS

I would like to thank Jenn Levo for her enthusiasm in drawing cartoons for this book, Jamison Green for sharing his expertise and encouragement, and Lauren Dockett, editor at Columbia University Press, for seeing value in this work. I would also like to thank my family and friends who have always supported me; without you, this book would not be possible.

TRANSGENDER

101

1

WHAT DOES IT MEAN TO BE TRANSGENDER?

An Introduction to the Term

What does it mean to be transgender? Think about yourself for a moment. How do you know that you are the gender you are? What makes you a woman or a man?[1] At first glance, the answer might seem simple.

Let's start with men. Maybe you think what makes you a man is your physical anatomy—your sex organs and secondary sex characteristics. Seems reasonable. But let's say that an unfortunate accident leaves you without one or more of these organs. You can no longer produce sperm. You're still a man, right? The question again: how do you know?

Maybe you think it's the large amount of testosterone in your body compared to females. But what if tomorrow your testosterone level dropped significantly? What if a female had a higher level than you? Chromosomes aren't foolproof, either. Stay with me. You're still a man, right? How do you know?

Let's move on to women. Perhaps you know you are a woman because you have given birth to a child. But what if you hadn't? What about before you did so? Were you unsure of your gender until you got pregnant? My guess is probably not. Maybe you point to menstruation.

Is it possible to be a woman and not menstruate? Sure. You've always known you were a woman. What we've just said is true of men is true of women, too. It's not because of your physical anatomy or your chromosomal makeup or the fact that the doctor pronounced you female at birth. Do you have an answer yet? How do you know you're a woman?

Suddenly these seemingly simple questions aren't so simple. Who you're attracted to, the toys you played with as a child, the clothes you wear now, your ability to process emotion or think analytically—all of these could be true of someone who is of the "opposite" gender. ("Opposite" is in quotation marks because as you will see, gender exists on a continuum; there may be two ends opposite each other, but there is so much more in between.)

By now you may be yelling out loud, "I just know! I've always known!" Well, that is probably the truest answer you can give. The proof of what gender you are lies within your brain.

DEFINING TRANSGENDERISM

The root of the word *transgender* comes from the Latin word *trans*, meaning "across." A transatlantic flight goes across the Atlantic Ocean; a transnational issue affects people all across the country; and so on. Transgender literally means "across gender."

Transgender is defined today as an umbrella term with many different identities existing under it. Some of these identities, such as *gender-variant*, *genderqueer*, and *cross-dresser*, are covered in chapter 8. We are going to put those aside for now. The type of transgenderism that we are most concerned with in the bulk of this book is *transsexualism*.

Many people see the term *transsexual* as dated, perhaps akin to calling a gay or lesbian person "homosexual." However, many people still use it to describe themselves. What is most important as you read this book is to keep in mind that transgender and transsexual are not exactly interchangeable.

By and large, *transsexual* refers to a person who identifies as the opposite sex of that which he or she was assigned at birth. *Transgender*, on the other hand, includes transsexual people, but the term also encompasses many more identities that are discussed later in the book. Many people use the terms transgender and transsexual interchangeably, but on a technical level this is incorrect. All transsexual people are transgender, but not all transgender people are transsexual.

An analogy to simplify things: transsexual is to transgender as Kleenex is to tissue. When you think about tissues (transgender people), Kleenex (transsexual people) is the most popular brand that comes to mind. Some people even call tissues Kleenexes. But tissues come in many other brands, and it is important to remember that, for instance, Puffs are not Kleenexes. They are Puffs; they are a type of tissue. If you were the CEO of Puffs and someone who worked for you asked you to hand her a Kleenex, you would probably be irritated and want to correct her. But again, for simplicity's sake, the brand of transgender people we refer to throughout the book is transsexual, unless otherwise specified. This includes the usage of the abbreviation "trans." So, think "Kleenex" until you get to chapter 8, where we discuss other "store brands."

Contrary to popular belief, being transsexual does not necessarily mean that someone has "changed sex." Confusing, I know. It does not require surgery or any medical intervention for that matter. Many transsexual people undergo surgery and hormone treatments, but some do not, for economic or other personal reasons. Surgery or other medical interventions are not what legitimize someone's transsexuality.

Language is a very important tool to us as human beings. You may have realized this when you had trouble answering the question at the beginning of this chapter. It is important to point out that every transperson has his or her own journey; just as a book about African American heritage doesn't speak to every single African American person's history, this book does not seek to describe every transperson's experience. This book speaks in general terms.

SEX VERSUS GENDER

Merriam-Webster defines sex and gender as the following:

> Sex: either of the two major forms of individuals that occur in many species and that are distinguished respectively as female or male especially on the basis of their reproductive organs and structures.[2]
>
> Gender: the behavioral, cultural, or psychological traits typically associated with one sex.[3]

Let's focus on the relationship that the dictionary has drawn between gender and sex. After all, this is what we have always been taught. If I am female (sex), then I am a woman (gender). If I am male, then I am a man. It seems to fit that logic statement we learned in grade school: if P, then Q. Right? Well, actually, life isn't quite that neat and simple. It is difficult to try to get components of human identity to fit perfectly into a logic equation. For many people, the link between gender and sex, as it is defined above, does not fit. For others, it fits perfectly.

We just learned that someone's transsexuality is not necessarily defined by surgery. Sex is not fully explained by its dictionary definition. According to some people, organs and structures do not dictate someone's sex just as they do not dictate someone's gender. For example, if someone asked a female-to-male transgender person what sex he was, he would likely respond "male," regardless of the fact that he might still have typically female organs. So, if someone feels that he is a man (gender), he would likely also consider himself male (sex). The key when talking about sex is differentiating between what sex people are labeled with at birth and what sex they consider themselves to be now.

Most transpeople feel that their gender differs from the sex they were labeled with at birth. Why that is, we have yet to figure out. But it doesn't much matter. The reality is that gender identity and sex line up differently from person to person. You might wonder why I am using the term "labeled with at birth." I don't always use this term, but you will definitely see it throughout the rest of the book. I use it because many transpeople feel that they were born the gender that they identify as; in other words, a male-to-female transperson might say that she was biologically always female, because her brain was wired to be that way, and the brain is part of biology. So, instead of always saying "born male" to refer to someone like her, I might differentiate by saying that she was "labeled male at birth" by a doctor, midwife, parents, and so on. Other terms that are becoming more common are *affirmed female,* someone who identifies as female but was not labeled female at birth, and *affirmed male,* someone who identifies as male but was not labeled male at birth.

Gender is a social construction. In most of Western society, children born male (sex) are expected to behave like boys and then men (gender), which means a host of things from playing with certain toys to assuming certain roles as an adult to refraining from showing too much emotion, and so on. There are hundreds—even thousands—of traits that our society puts in the "male" column or the "female" column, and not too many overlap. This is simply not realistic for everyday life, and it never has been.

THE GENDER BINARY

Merriam-Webster defines the word binary as "something made of or based on two things or parts."[4] The gender binary is a social system whereby people are thought to have either of two genders: man or woman. These genders are expected to correspond to birth sex: male or female. In the gender binary system, there is no room for interpretation, for living between genders, or for crossing the binary. The gender binary system is rigid and restrictive for many people who feel that their natal sex (the sex they were labeled with at birth) does not match up with their gender or that their gender is fluid and not fixed.

The gender binary exists for easy categorization and labeling purposes. For most people, it is something that is taken for granted. People who are not transgender—meaning those whose gender identity does match up with their birth sex—often naturally accept the gender binary system as a given. Females who identify as women use the women's restroom. Males who identify as men dress in suits and ties or tuxedos for formal events. It is the way it is, and that fits well for many people. But for transpeople living in a culture where the gender binary rules all, it is a daily battle. We discuss some of these struggles later in the book.

SEX, GENDER IDENTITY, AND GENDER EXPRESSION

We have covered the main differences between sex and gender. Now we are going to divide gender into two parts: gender identity and gender expression. The University of Minnesota's Transgender Commission defines these terms as the following:

> Gender identity is one's internal sense of who they are; being a woman or man, girl or boy, or between or beyond these genders.
>
> Gender expression is the external representation of one's gender identity, usually expressed through feminine or masculine behaviors and signals such as clothing, hair, movement, voice or body characteristics.[5]

Some people may use the terms male and female for gender identity instead of or in addition to man and woman.

You may be familiar with the term *gender role*. Historically, a typical gender role for a man would be to work and be the breadwinner, while a woman's role would be to take care of the home and children. Gender roles are closely tied to gender expression. For simplicity's sake, we are going to leave the term gender role out and just concentrate on sex, gender identity, and gender expression. Table 1.1 shows the relationship between these three and the way the lineup is expected to occur (as dictated by our society).

For transpeople, this lineup does not occur. Any of the words in these boxes can be switched around. Chances are, whether you know it or not, you have come across someone of each and every possible combination.

Table 1.1

Sex	Gender Identity	Gender Expression
Female	Woman	Feminine
Male	Man	Masculine

Now place yourself in this table. At this moment, and at most moments, you might feel that you line up like one of the examples. But at other points, you might feel differently. For example: let's take a man, born male, who does multiple things on a given day. This man works in the construction industry, doing heavy lifting, operating a crane, and getting dirty. At work, it would seem that this man's sex, gender identity, and gender expression are lining up perfectly as table 1.1 shows. He is a man, born male, and is working a job that is typically deemed to be masculine. But when he gets home, he remembers that he needs to cook dinner for his wife who is returning from a business trip later in the evening. The man does so not thinking that anything has changed within him—even though cooking dinner for a spouse is a stereotypically feminine activity. As he moves from hands-on construction to putting on an apron and cooking a meal, his gender expression may be changing. He doesn't take conscious notice of this; for him, it's all in a day's work. On a continuum, his gender expression on that particular day might look like table 1.2. So, does that make him transgender? He might not think so; but remember, in the true sense of the word, he is moving "across" gender.

Out of the three terms—sex, gender identity, and gender expression—which do you think we notice most about people on a daily basis? If it were a person's sex, then we would have to see under that person's clothes or test his or her chromosomes (and even then we could get a conflicting report). If it were a person's gender identity, we would have to either ask that person how he or she identifies or somehow get inside the brain and find the answer for ourselves. By process of elimination, you guessed it: it's gender expression. As we learned from the ability to mix up the terms on the chart, someone's gender expression does not necessarily tell you what that person's sex or gender identity is. But, as

Table 1.2

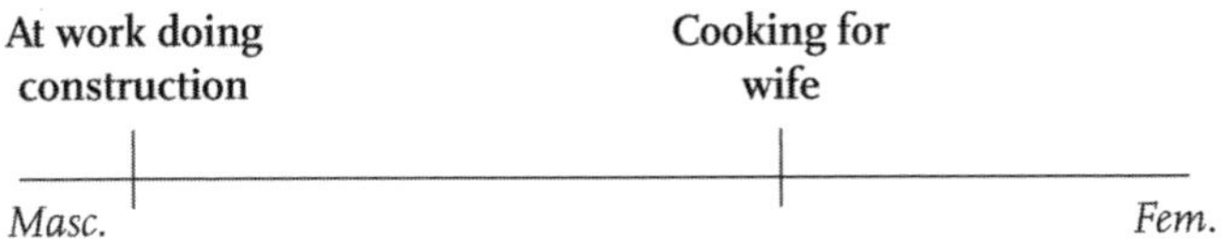

Figure 1.1: "You think you have problems! Try being a male ladybug."

Source: © *www.cartoonstock.com*

human beings, we tend to assume by looking at how people express themselves.

Here is an example: you see a person walking down the street with a short haircut wearing a shirt and tie and men's dress pants. The short haircut and outfit are typically signs of a masculine gender expression. Because you see this person's masculine gender expression with your own eyes, you fill out the chart in table 1.1 in your mind, assuming that this person identifies as a man and that he is anatomically male. But what if this person has been hiding a secret for many years? What if this person was indeed born male but feels like a woman inside and cannot, for various reasons, express that to the world? This is more common than you might think. That person's chart would look like table 1.3.

Table 1.3

Sex (Labeled at Birth)	Gender Identity	Gender Expression
Male	**Woman**	Masculine

It is only natural to assume. We need to make assumptions on a daily basis. We assume that a car will stop at a red light; we assume that the grocery store is stocked with the ingredients we will need for dinner; and we assume that the sun will rise and set. However, it is good to be aware that we are assuming people's gender identity on a daily basis. Inevitably there are times when our assumptions are wrong, whether or not we know it.

Here is one more example of a person whose chart is different than the majority: a female who identifies as a woman but who works as an auto mechanic and wears men's work clothes on a daily basis (table 1.4). Perhaps you know someone like this. Would this woman call herself transgender? Probably not, but again, in some ways she routinely moves across gender.

Table 1.4

Sex (Labeled at Birth)	Gender Identity	Gender Expression
Female	Woman	**Masculine**

Phrases I have heard again and again about transpeople include "She is really a man" or "He is really a woman." Now that you know about sex and gender identity, you know that this statement is false. "She was labeled male at birth, but is a woman" is correct (though without permission from this transperson herself, it is disrespectful to out her, or reveal that information).

Gender expression is not something that we normally allow our children to form for themselves. Let's think about babies for a moment. They are too young to decide how to express their gender, so their parents do it for them. I was in a baby store recently and overheard a woman (yes, I'm assuming she was a woman) say that she thought a soccer ball mobile was cute but the baby was going to be a girl, so she couldn't buy it. Along those same lines, what do people often dress baby boys in? Blue. If we think about why people do that, it is almost comical.

The baby boy must be dressed in blue so that strangers or acquaintances know that he is a boy and don't mistake him for a girl. Because this baby is dressed in blue, people will assume that he has a penis and a Y chromosome and that he will want to play with trucks, footballs, and army figurines. That's a lot of information for a parent to give simply by dressing a child in a specific color. If you asked his parents why they dressed him in blue, they probably wouldn't think of any of that. They might say, "Because he is a boy." The same is true for pink and baby girls.

Gender is a construction that is ingrained in us from day one of life, literally. What do we fear would happen if we purchased the soccer ball mobile for the baby girl? Might she grow up to be masculine? Might she be confused? Might people who enter her bedroom think that she was a boy or that her parents were crazy for buying a mobile that they liked without taking gender into consideration? What about baby girls who are still relatively bald and have bows wrapped around their heads? "Until her hair grows long," her parents might think, "we must make sure that everyone knows she is not a boy, so let's put a bow on her head."

Most people dress their babies in pink or blue because it seems practical. But no matter the reasons, the social ramifications are far reaching. You could probably stand on a street corner in a crowded city with a baby dressed in pink and get each and every person you saw to guess that the baby was a girl. For adults, it might not be only blue or pink, but clothing is still a major part of expression. This is difficult for those who do not feel comfortable with these norms, especially those who are trans.

WHICH TERM REFERS TO WHICH?

You may have heard someone called a *transwoman* or *transman*. What does that mean exactly? When using these terms, you should always go with the gender with which someone identifies. For instance, a transman/transguy is usually someone who was labeled female at birth but now identifies as a man or a male. Transmen, most of whom use the pronoun "he," should always be addressed as such. You are describing someone as the gender that person is—not the gender that person was assigned at birth. The opposite obviously goes for transwomen. The term transwoman is usually used as a descriptor for someone who was labeled male at birth but now identifies as a woman or a female.

Another set of commonly used terms are: *FTM* (or *F2M*) and *MTF* (or *M2F*). The former stands for female-to-male transperson and the latter is a male-to-female transperson. Transwoman and MTF/M2F can usually be used interchangeably. The same is true for transman/ transguy and FTM/F2M.

You might have heard people use the word *transgendered.* Some people feel that it makes them sound like an object rather than a person. Generally transgender is sufficient as an adjective in the sentence "he is transgender" or "he is a transgender person." If you are looking for a verb, use *transition.* "He transitioned from female to male," not "he transgendered from female to male."

PRONOUNS

One of the biggest challenges people face when addressing or talking about trans individuals is the use of pronouns. What to use: he, him, his, she, her, hers, they, their, theirs? Perhaps you've thought about trying not to use a pronoun at all. It sounds difficult and complicated, but there is one element to it that people often overlook. Something else our society has taught us is that it is rude to ask people personal questions. Sometimes, though, it can make things much easier. After age ten or so, it is not considered permissible to ask an adult if he or she is a "man or a woman." But we can't all be psychics. It is permissible, and even preferred in some cases, to ask—just not in the same way a ten-year-old might.

Consider this: most people who present *androgynously* (meaning, in this case, that it is unclear what their sex and/or gender might be) are aware that they present as such. Instead of letting the question of gender distract you from a conversation you might be having with someone, begin by asking what pronoun that person prefers to use. It may sound strange, but it is helpful in many situations. If someone asked you what pronoun you prefer, you might give that person a puzzled look. But someone who lives his/her/their/etc. life appearing to be near the middle of the gender spectrum might appreciate being asked what is the preferred pronoun. Asking shows a level of respect and comfort. At least then you won't be preoccupied with trying not to offend this person, and you can concentrate on the conversation at hand.

Pronouns can be a bit more complicated than just *he* or *she*. Because we know gender is on a continuum, in a way, pronouns are, too. The vast majority of trans and nontrans individuals use he or she. Some people may prefer *their* (used as a singular pronoun) or a host of other words. It can be very difficult to remember to use nontraditional pronouns, but it is important to respect people's wishes.

One of the hardest things for people to do is change the pronoun of someone they have known for a long time. If you work with, teach, parent, or just generally know a person as "she" for many years, it is very difficult to immediately adjust to calling him "he" even if that is who he feels he is. There is a happy medium between feeling guilty that you can only get the new pronoun correct 85 percent of the time and refusing to attempt to use the preferred pronoun at all. If someone you know has changed pronouns from she to he or vice versa, try as best you can to use the preferred pronoun, but give yourself some room to make mistakes here and there. You will get better with time and practice. If you do not live with the person, practice using the new pronoun with other people and you will find that it comes naturally the more you do it. It's like almost anything else; you can train yourself.

It is also important for transpeople to remember that even if their friends and loved ones are trying, they are still bound to make mistakes from time to time. Many transpeople have to make the switch in their own head and may themselves slip. One common misconception is that as the person who is now "she" begins to look more feminine in appearance, you will never again make a pronoun mistake. But a mistake can happen at any time. It is not a reflection on what the person now looks like. It is because old habits die hard, and the first gender we know for a person is what sticks in our mind until such time as we can completely train it to change. For some people it takes longer than others. Some people will slip, out of the blue, twenty years after someone begins transitioning and wonder where that came from. Just correct yourself and move on. After all, if you are referring to a transwoman as "he" in public, and she looks like any other female, people will begin to give *you* funny looks. Pronouns are indeed an important part of the English language. Tell a short story about your best friend, out loud, trying not to use pronouns. Easy? Not quite.

TRANSGENDER BY THE NUMBERS

Unfortunately there is no major consensus on the number of transgender people in the United States or the world today. Estimates of transsexual people in the 1970s were 1 in 37,000 transsexual women (MTFs) out of the general population and 1 in 107,000 transsexual men (FTMs) out of the general population.[6] Today, estimates of the transsexual population are somewhere between .25 percent and 1 percent of the U.S. population[7] (a pretty big range) and numbers of the larger transgender population are thought to be greater than that. Hard-and-fast statistics are lacking for a couple of reasons. One is that many transpeople are not out and are either living as trans behind closed doors or are living *stealth*ily, meaning that people do not know that they were born differently than they appear now.

Another reason for the lack of statistics is that so many different varieties of transgenderism fall under the umbrella term that it is hard to discern which subcategories should actually be statistically counted as transgender and which should not. For example, male cross-dressers, who don't live their lives as full-time women, are completely different from transsexual women who do live their lives as full-time women. Should they be lumped together because they fall under the umbrella of transgenderism? Some say yes, some say no. Social stigma keeps us from getting accurate numbers for this population. Yet without statistics, the population remains invisible. It is an unfortunate cycle.

By this point you have figured out that the subject of transgenderism includes a little bit of grammar, a basic understanding of biology, a lot of sociology, a lesson in history, some critical analysis, and a hint of language origin. Let's move on to learn about the differences between sexual orientation and gender.

2

SEXUAL ORIENTATION VERSUS GENDER

What's the Difference?

First of all, let's figure out what we mean by sexual orientation and gender. *Sexual orientation* relates to someone's romantic and sexual attraction to another person. One may be attracted to a person of a different gender, the same gender, "both" or all genders, or to no one at all. *Gender identity* is an inner sense of being a man, woman, neither, somewhere in between, and so on. It does not necessarily correspond with the sex one is labeled with at birth, as is the case with transpeople. *Gender expression* is how people dress and carry themselves, whether it be in a masculine, feminine, or in-between way. So, is sexual orientation connected to gender identity and expression at all? Yes, in several ways. Are they the same things? Definitely not.

Since the acronym *GLBT* (for gay, lesbian, bisexual, or transgender, sometimes written as LGBT) became mainstream, confusion has ensued. The use of GLBT is good because it has made B and T more widely known than they were before. However, T is often lost in the shuffle. Many people have picked up GLBT as a direct replacement for the phrase "gay and lesbian." But, as we know, understanding transgenderism as distinct from sexual orientation is important. Some GLBT groups have added "transgender" to "gay and lesbian" but they haven't changed anything internally, so essentially they are still gay and lesbian–focused groups. Hopefully you can be one of the growing number of people who lets others know that GLB, which refer to sexual orientation, are not the same as transgender, which relates to gender.

THE BASICS

How do you identify your gender? Man? Woman? Transgender? Something else? More than one of the above? Well, it could be any combination. As we know, if you are transgender then you do not identify exclusively with the biological sex you were labeled with at birth. If you are not transgender, however, and you *do* identify with the biological sex you were labeled with at birth, then you might be called nontransgender or *cisgender*. The prefix *cis* is derived from Latin and essentially means "same." Your gender identity is the same as your birth sex. If you were born male, you identify as a man. The vast majority of people are cisgender. Some people prefer nontransgender over cisgender and vice versa.

Now, what is your sexual orientation? Heterosexual/straight, gay, lesbian, bisexual, pansexual, asexual? Let's get some quick definitions: *heterosexual* or *straight* people are romantically attracted to people of the opposite sex from themselves. *Gay* people are attracted to people of the same sex, and the term can be used to describe men and women. *Lesbians* are women attracted to other women. *Bisexual* people are attracted to men and women. Here are two less well-known ones: *pansexual* people are attracted to people of any and all genders, not just men or women, and *asexual* people generally do not experience romantic attraction toward other people at all. These are all types of sexual orientations, but they are not the only sexual orientations.

Let's map out what we've just talked about. Using only the most common sexual orientations (straight, gay, bi) and gender identities

Table 2.1

Gender ID	Non-trans man	Non-trans woman	Transman	Transwoman
Sexual Orientation				
Straight	x	x	x	x
Gay/Lesbian	x	x	x	x
Bisexual	x	x	x	x

(non-trans man, non-trans woman, transman, transwoman), we can create a chart (table 2.1).

An X marks each possibility. Non-trans men may be straight, gay, bisexual, and so on. Transmen may also be straight, gay, bisexual, and so on. So, what would a gay transman be like? Remember that trans-people are referred to as the gender they identify as, so transmen are men who were labeled female at birth. A gay transman, therefore, is attracted to men. A lesbian transwoman is attracted to women, and so on. Of course, since we are dealing with people, it's not quite that simple. You might have thought that, for instance, all transmen were lesbians prior to transition. Not so. There are many transmen who are attracted to men and the same is true for transwomen and women. In fact, any sexual orientation for any person at any point in time is possible. On to the next word: *queer*.

QUEER: AN OLD TERM WITH A NEW MEANING

Queer used to be a derogatory term (and still is, in some contexts) used by non-GLBT people toward GLBT people. "He's such a queer" or "what are you, queer or something?" were phrases often used along with the terms *faggot* and *dyke* (derogatory words for a gay man and a lesbian, respectively). But now, queer has been "taken back" by—well—the queer community. Queer is an easy catchall word for those who are gay, lesbian, bisexual, transgender, questioning their sexuality, or otherwise do not fit into the heterosexual or male/female binary worlds. It is easier than saying GLBTQ. At this point the word is still touchy for many people because it has such a negative history, and it is most often used by younger generations. So, use the term *queer* with caution.

How does this tie into the differences between gender identity and sexual orientation? Well, queer does lump GLB in with T and others, but in this case it can be a more comfortable way for someone to identify without explaining that he is a gay transman or a straight transman. For example, a transman who is attracted to women could be defined as straight. However, if a transman does not feel comfortable identifying as straight because it erases his past and his identity in a way, he might identify as just queer. Same goes for a gay transman who might not feel that "gay" defines all of who he is because of his transgenderism. If someone tells you he or she is queer, that won't define the person's gender identity or sexual orientation for you, but it will tell you that he or she identifies somewhere in the GLBT community. In other words, if you look at table 2.1, people who fall into any of the six Xs under Transman and Transwoman could identify as queer. Likewise, many GLB people are increasingly choosing to identify as queer instead of just gay, lesbian,

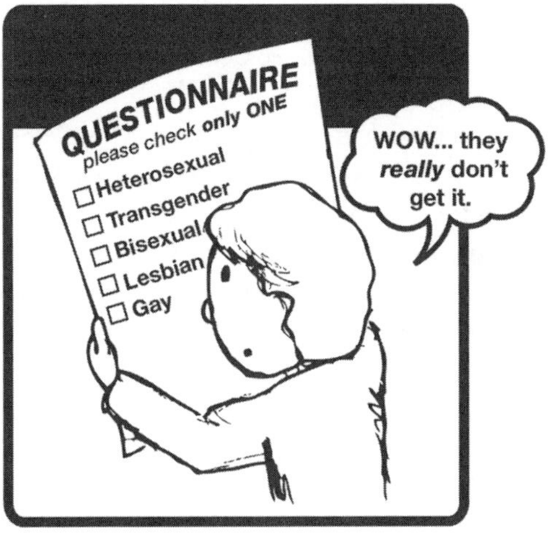

Figure 2.1

Source: © *2010 Jennifer Levo. Text of cartoons by Nicholas M. Teich*

or bisexual. Even allies to the queer community can identify on the queer spectrum. It's all a personal choice. It is important to know that some transpeople will identify as straight, gay, bi, and so forth, and not queer, but some will identify as queer.

THE KINSEY SCALE OF SEXUAL ORIENTATION

Developed in 1948 by Dr. Alfred Kinsey, sexologist at Indiana University, the Kinsey Scale measures sexual orientation along a continuum.[1] Zero on the scale denotes exclusive attraction to the opposite sex/gender, or complete heterosexuality. A three on the scale is assigned to a person attracted equally to men and women, and a six means exclusive attraction to the same gender/sex, or complete homosexuality. Table 2.2 is a bare-bones look at the Kinsey Scale.

By gathering research over many years from average people across the country, Kinsey and his colleagues got what most considered to be unexpected results in the 1940s. He and his team came to theorize that many people fall somewhere in between zero and six and are not actually *at* zero or six. This is still widely believed today. (Whether or not many people will admit at least some attraction to the same sex is a different story.) Kinsey and his colleagues released these findings and lots of other interesting (though taboo at the time) information in the 1948 book *Sexual Behavior in the Human Male*, which was followed by *Sexual Behavior in the Human Female* in 1953.[2]

Remember, anyone of any gender can fall anywhere on the Kinsey Scale. It does not matter whether you are a transwoman or a non-trans man or anywhere in between. The Kinsey Scale is only about your sexual behavior/attraction, not about what gender you are.

Table 2.2

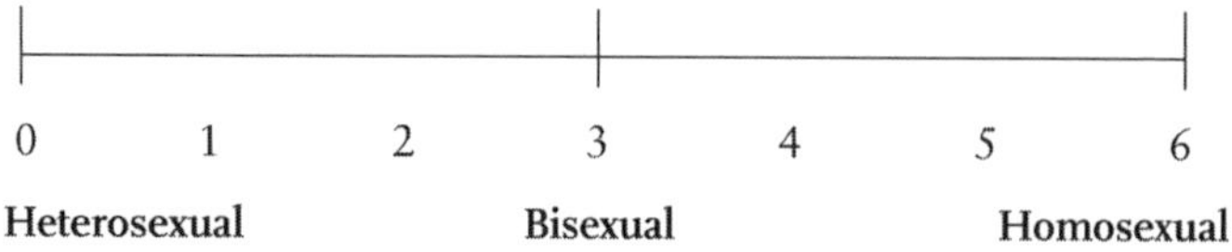

GENDER IDENTITY AND EXPRESSION CONTINUA

Just as sexual orientation lies on a continuum, so too does gender identity. Some people feel that they are a combination of different genders, not just man or woman. Table 2.3 is a simple version of a gender identity continuum.

Table 2.3

Cisgender/ Non-trans	**Genderqueer**	**Transsexual**

Where do you fall? Sometimes it depends on the day, but most people fall closer to the cisgender or non-trans side of the scale. That being said, societal restrictions keep people from expressing—or talking about—mixed-gender feelings they might have. This is part of the reason it is so difficult to get a specific figure on how many transpeople exist.

Table 2.4 shows a rudimentary continuum of gender expression. Where you fall in this continuum might depend not only on the day but on a specific time on a specific day. We talked about this in chapter 1 when we went over gender expression's link to gender identity. As you will see, it is most often gender expression that gets mixed up with—or is sometimes closely aligned with—sexual orientation.

Table 2.4

Masculine	**Feminine**

CONNECTING THE DOTS

So, if gender identity is the gender you are and sexual orientation is the gender(s) you are attracted to, then why are the two terms connected at all? Perhaps Annamarie Jagose and Don Kulick put it best in their 2004 article "Thinking Sex/Thinking Gender": "Of course, the correct relation between sexuality and gender can never be definitively specified. One of the enduring motivations of LGBT . . . is precisely its inability to pin down that relation or—to put it otherwise—our ceaseless imagining of it in new ways."[3]

Like many subjects in this book, there is no quick and easy answer. What we will do, however, is explore some of the similarities and differences between sexual orientation and gender.

Have you ever walked down the street and seen a masculine-looking woman with short hair, no makeup, wearing typical men's clothing, walking in what might be perceived as a masculine manner, and thought, "Oh, she's definitely a lesbian"? Let's assume you have. Take that example: a masculine-looking woman assumed to be a lesbian. We are going to assume this is a female who identifies as a woman. What is it about her that is telling us she's a lesbian? It is her gender expression. She is expressing herself in a masculine way. Now why does that set off lesbian buzzers in our minds? Well, especially in the media, lesbians are often portrayed as masculine. In fact, we have seen the butch-femme couple, in which one is masculine and one is feminine, many times on television and in movies. (While in some lesbian couples one presents as masculine and one as feminine, lesbian couples may express their gender in an infinite number of ways.) But when we see that butch, masculine woman, we have been told to think that she is expressing herself in a masculine manner because she is "like a man," which in turn helps us to make sense of why she is attracted to women. This is not true. Butch or masculine-looking lesbians are by and large cisgender (non-trans). They do not want to be men or even be like men. If they did, then they might consider themselves transgender men and not lesbians, and they might take steps to live as men. Remember that gender identity (in this case, a woman) and gender expression (in this case, masculine) does not automatically mean anything about a person's sexual orientation.

Let's go back to the moment when we see this masculine-looking woman on the street. What if she is walking arm in arm with a man and is holding a small child's hand? Might we change our perception of "definite lesbian" to think, "Hey, that (straight) woman looks really masculine"? There are all sorts of heterosexual women who like to express themselves in a masculine manner. At the same time, there are all sorts of lesbian women who express themselves in a feminine manner and wouldn't be caught dead in a baseball cap or an oxford shirt. The perception of butch as the only way for a lesbian to be has changed over the last century. Television shows like Showtime's *The L Word* that portray feminine lesbians are becoming more mainstream. In the 1920s, it was believed that all lesbians should look very masculine; there was hardly a place for feminine gay women.[4]

Masculine woman does not necessarily equal lesbian, and lesbian does not necessarily equal masculine woman. However, there may be a connection between some lesbians and a more masculine gender expression. But perhaps just as many women who present in a feminine way are lesbian, too. Those people just don't set off our *gaydar*—as in radar, a sense that someone is gay—because they are expressing in a feminine way and thus blending in with other women.

Now think about feminine men. They may express themselves in a feminine manner by the way they dress, carry themselves, speak, walk, and so on. Straight women might perceive such men as less threatening because they think the men are gay. Likewise, straight men might perceive such men as *more* threatening because they think that feminine men are gay. But again, this perception—this gaydar—is based on gender expression only, until such a man declares his sexual orientation as gay (or bisexual, etc.). In the last twenty years or so, a term popped up to include straight men whose gender expression is more feminine than that of the stereotypical straight man—*metrosexual*. Metrosexuals often dress fashionably or fastidiously. How are we to tell a gay man from a straight, metrosexual man? Until someone lets you know his sexual orientation, you are left to assume for yourself.

Many people make assumptions about sexual orientation based on gender expression. It is human nature to make assumptions, as I previously mentioned. But it is considered rude to ask whether someone is gay, bisexual, or something else. Until the new coworker tells us that he has a husband or boyfriend or wife or girlfriend, we might be inclined, because of what we've always been taught, to assume that his feminine manner means that he is gay. In this case the key is to recognize that our assumption lies simply in gender expression and not in any other evidence of actual sexual orientation.

If you have ever seen the 1996 Mike Nichols film *The Birdcage*, which is based on the French play *La Cage aux Folles*, then you know that Robin Williams (Armand) and Nathan Lane (Albert) play a gay couple whose son is getting married to a conservative senator's daughter, and they have to find a way to pretend that they are not gay when the senator and his family come over to meet them for dinner. They decide that Albert will try to play the role of their son's uncle rather than one of his fathers. There is a memorable scene in which Armand is teaching Albert, a gay man who performs as a drag queen, how to act masculine to pull off his role as the straight uncle. Albert has a very feminine gender expression, so the challenge of getting him to seem straight seems insurmountable. This scene exemplifies the blurred lines between gender and sexuality. Why will the senator's family figure out that Albert is gay simply by meeting him? The thought is that his feminine ways will tip them off; his nonmasculine gender expression will give away his sexual orientation.

At least a couple of forces, beyond gender expression, link GLBT people together. One is activism. We've all heard the expression "safety in numbers." Well, take that a step further. The more people are involved in a cause, the more likely it is to progress, and more quickly, at that. Second, *drag queens* (historically, gay men dressed as women, usually for performances) and transwomen were a large part of the Stonewall rebellion, which set off the gay rights movement; without them, the movement might never have taken off like it did. We will learn more about Stonewall in chapter 5.

ORIENTATION AND GENDER STEREOTYPES

Lesbians just want to be men and gay men just want to be women, right?

This is an area where people conflate sexual orientation with gender identity all the time. We touched on this a bit already but the point is worth repeating. Lesbians are women who are sexually or romantically attracted to women. The key is that they are women. Gay men are men who are attracted to other men. They are men and wish to remain men. People who might think that gay people really want to be the opposite sex are seeing the world in a *heteronormative* way; that is to say, they believe that heterosexuality is the norm and perhaps the only way to be. They are judging gay people against the norm of heterosexuality. Therefore, if a woman likes women, to be "normal," she would have to want to become a man. This is simply not true, which is why it is important to differentiate between sexual orientation and gender identity.

If we look at society as a diverse group of individuals where heterosexuality might be most common but not necessarily normal, then we can more easily see that human sexual orientation varies; some people happen to be straight, some gay, some bisexual, some pansexual, and so on. This does not necessarily have anything to do with a person's gender identity or expression.

Some people do believe that transitioning genders is preferable to being gay. In other words, if you are a man who likes men, then you should just become a woman and call it a day. It would be easier in the long run. Many things are wrong with this statement, but heternormativity is so pervasive throughout the world that some believe this to be a better option. This would be like asking any nontransperson to transition genders. Let's assume that we lived in a "homonormative" world and you were a woman who was attracted to men. You would be pressured to become a man so that you would be normal; a man who likes men. It might sound absurd when put this way, but it is only really as absurd as it is to ask a non-trans gay person to change genders to fit into a heteronormative society.

On the flip side, some believe that transgender or transsexual people aren't really trans, they just transitioned because they were too ashamed to be gay. In other words, they felt the need to blend into our heteronormative society and that is the sole reason for the gender transition. This is another misunderstanding. Remember the table with the Xs marking different possibilities and combinations of gender identities and sexual orientations? For nonheterosexual transpeople (that is, post-transition), this theory of transitioning to become heterosexual obviously does not work. It does not work for transpeople who are heterosexual post-transition, either. This is because, again, there is a distinct difference between sexual orientation and gender identity. If people change gender (think about all the lifelong implications of doing so) simply because they do not want to be seen as gay, then they would be living a lie just like any nontransperson who tried to change gender.

GLBT PEOPLE DON'T ALWAYS HAVE SOLIDARITY

Judith Halberstam, author and professor at the University of Southern California, has done a lot of research and writing on the subject of what she calls "border wars": the gray area between butch women, most of whom are lesbians, and FTMs.

"Some lesbians seem to see FTMs as traitors to a 'women's' movement who cross over and become the enemy. Some FTMs see lesbian feminism as a discourse that has demonized them and their masculinity. Some butches consider FTMs to be butches who 'believe in anatomy,' and some FTMs consider butches to be FTMs who are too afraid to transition."[5]

The divide between butch lesbians and FTMs is an interesting one. Many lesbians work tirelessly for trans rights and accept FTMs as their brethren, and vice versa. However, as Halberstam points out, many lesbians and FTMs are at odds. (It might seem strange that one marginalized group expends any energy bringing down another, but this is practiced by groups of all kinds.) The idea that men have always been afforded more privilege in our society is a large part of why women and their allies continue to work toward true equality between men and women. When a "woman" becomes a man (woman is in quotes because many FTMs never identify as women to begin with), especially since the internal process that transpeople go through is not well understood, it can evoke feelings of anger, disgust, and even betrayal. Women who have worked toward equal rights and against male domination can feel especially angry toward FTMs. However, many FTMs have worked toward women's equal rights before transition and continue to do so after transition. The voices of FTMs who pass as men to the general public can be especially helpful on women's issues.

At the same time, there are FTMs who once occupied lesbian spaces who do not want to have anything to do with the lesbian community, or even the greater GLBT community, after they transition. They want to fit seamlessly into society as men, end of discussion. These FTMs may have some contempt toward the lesbian and GLBT communities. Although living *stealth* (not out as trans) is very important for some transpeople, it does not excuse disdain toward the greater GLBT community.

As we know, not all FTMs were lesbians prior to transition. There may be more FTMs who come from the lesbian community than MTFs who come from the gay male community, but I do not know of any valid statistics on the subject. Transmen who were formerly "straight women" may be slower to integrate into the GLBT community because they were not part of it before, and the same goes for transwomen who used to identify as straight and now might identify as lesbian, queer, or anything of the sort. These people may find the gay, lesbian, and bisexual communities to be less welcoming.

Not many people have studied or written about the border between gay men and MTFs. As mentioned above, perhaps this is because a large percentage of MTFs were "straight men" prior to transition, and thus they are not faced with the same issues as the large number of FTMs who were formerly lesbians. There are tensions between non-trans women of all sexual orientations and transwomen over what some call "women-born-women-only" (sometimes spelled womyn-born-womyn) spaces, which are places where only non-trans women are welcome. This begins to stray from our topic of sexual orientation versus gender, as it raises the question "Who is to say what gender someone is?" which is altogether a fascinating area. I encourage those who are interested to learn more about it.

Some lesbian and gay people are at odds with transpeople on the topic of marriage. While gay couples are making strides in marriage equality with straight couples, the battle is still far from over. Transpeople who used to be gay identified but are now straight identified (post-transition) can marry freely like any other heterosexual couple. This can evoke feelings of resentment from the gay and lesbian community.[6]

You might wonder what happens when someone transitions from male to female while dating or married to a woman. What happens to both partners' sexual orientations if they decide to stay together? This is a complicated question, and the bottom line is that it is personal for everyone. There is not one universal answer. Let's say that in this case, the nontransitioning partner always considered herself straight. Now that her partner is MTF, she is with a woman. Is she a lesbian? If she weren't with this woman, would she want to be with a man? Well, yes, most likely, if she has always identified as straight. But now when she walks down the street with her partner they will inevitably be seen as a lesbian couple. This is something that many people grapple with when a partner transitions genders. What about the transitioning partner? Does she go from being seen as a straight man to identifying as a lesbian? Quite possibly. Again, it depends on how each person wants to work it out. You might say that society dictates that this is now a lesbian couple, case closed. Then again, unfortunately, there are people who will never legitimize someone's gender identity post-transition and will always think of an MTF person as a man and vice versa for someone who is FTM.

What about a lesbian relationship in which one of the partners transitions to male? What happens to the lesbian identity of each partner? Some women whose partners transition from female to male still retain a lesbian identity. Some may say that this is impossible; if she is with a man, then she is not a lesbian. There are transmen who feel that it is an affront to their identity as a man to have a female partner who retains her lesbian identity. However, some people keep their lesbian identity as a political and community identity, and not so much a sexual orientation. What about a straight relationship in which the "woman" transitions to male? Does this person's partner go from a straight man to a gay man?

These are questions commonly asked of transgender people. However, if you would not normally ask them of a nontransperson, then do not assume it is all right to ask them of a transperson. Many people feel that sexual orientation is fluid and that love transcends sex and gender boundaries. After all, as we saw with the Kinsey Scale, many people are not exclusively either homosexual or heterosexual.

When we bring marriage into the picture, things can get complicated. Is transgender marriage the same as gay marriage? Well, considering what we've learned so far in this chapter, hopefully your answer is: it depends. Is the couple a same-sex couple now that one (or more) of the partners has transitioned? If yes, then it's gay marriage. If no, then it's not. Generally people do not ask for proof of your sex when you go to get a marriage license. It's a given that when a couple wants to get married, and it looks like the couple is made up of a man and a woman, then that is legal. Therefore, if a heterosexual couple—where one partner is trans—tries to get married, if they pass as a heterosexual couple, they'll get the green light. The subject of sex and gender identity is not on most people's radar. If something tips someone off, like a driver's license with a sex marker that differs from the person's appearance, then confusion ensues. If you are a heterosexual transwoman whose driver's license is marked M, for whatever reason, and you try to marry a man in a state where same-sex marriage is not legal, you may run into a problem. Conversely, if you are a lesbian-identified transwoman who was legally married to a woman prior to transition, some people may claim your union is now illegal because it is presently a same-sex marriage.

This subject has come up in a few court cases in the United States. In Virginia in 2008, a transwoman and non-trans man got married after filling out a marriage license application with spaces for the bride's and groom's names. Officials later found out that the bride was a transwoman, whom they did not deem to be a "real" woman, and tried to bring the couple up on charges of fraud. The city's prosecutor could not prove that the definition of the terms "bride" and "groom" were limited to a male and a female, so charges were never brought. However, in light of this case, the state swiftly changed the marriage license forms to read "male applicant" and "female applicant."[7] This subject brings up the question of which piece of identification makes someone's sex or gender valid. Is it a driver's license? A passport? What if several different identifications have different gender markers on them? Who is to say that the bride in this case, a transwoman, is not really a woman? What about someone who is not 100 percent biologically “male” or “female” who tries to get married? Who is to judge what sex a person is? These questions are difficult ones that continue to plague the transgender community.

Now that we have a grip on the differences and similarities between gender and sexual orientation, let’s look at what it means to come out as a transgender person.

3

COMING OUT AS TRANSGENDER

When, Why, and How People Come Out

Coming out, or revealing one's transgenderism, can be one of the most difficult parts of a transperson's journey. At the same time, it can be one of the proudest and most satisfying. But before transpeople can come out to others, they must come out to themselves. For some people, the process of coming out never really ends, but it becomes easier with practice and time. Other people who come out initially choose not to identify as trans at all, and they identify simply as the gender they feel they are: man, woman, and so forth.

WHY COME OUT?

The simplest answer: to be yourself, to live life as the genuine you, it's necessary to come out in at least some areas of life. We usually hear the term "coming out," which is the short form of "coming out of the closet," in reference to sexual orientation. While certainly not ideal, it is possible for most gay, lesbian, and bisexual people to go through their daily lives without revealing to whom they are sexually attracted or with whom they might have a romantic relationship. However, transpeople have a different set of circumstances. Once they begin any type of transition that makes them look different from the sex they were labeled with at birth, their gender-nonconforming appearance is plain for all to see. Thus, the choice of whether to come out is not readily available to most transpeople, at least in the beginning of transition.

COMING OUT TO SELF

Realization that one is trans can take anywhere from a few moments to several decades. Usually transpeople have an inkling early on in their lives that their assigned gender feels out of whack with their bodies. The self-realization process is extremely complicated. The human mind does its best to help us survive, which can translate into triggering intense denial. Because of societal constraints, it is common for a person to try to ignore signs pointing toward transgenderism, whether consciously or unconsciously.

Deana F. Morrow, editor and contributing writer for *Sexual Orientation and Gender Expression in Social Work Practice*, notes, "Being [trans] does not automatically make a person immune to the pejorative terms and misinformation used to construct images and stereotypes of GLBT people. GLBT people tend to internalize those messages, and they have to 'unlearn' much of that harmful rhetoric."[1] This is known as internalized homophobia for GLB people and internalized transphobia for transpeople. Those who do recognize that they have been raised as the wrong gender may still not know that transition is available to them or even that it exists at all. Let's consider the following analogy: if a person falls down and lands on her wrist, and her wrist swells painfully, then she will likely visit a doctor or hospital. She will get an X-ray that will confirm what happened: broken, sprained, and so on. Transgenderism just isn't that simple. Although there may be signs throughout someone's life, being trans is not on most people's minds. Transpeople are not born with sensors that pop up one day and tell them that they are trans. It is not like a broken wrist; it is not something that says, "Hey, you fell. You're in pain. Go get an X-ray!"

Each person has a different level of self-awareness for a variety of reasons. Many transpeople realize that they are different from their peers at an early age, but some do not know why they feel this way. Some feel that they are nonconforming in many ways while others clearly identify that they are different in terms of gender. The stage that follows this initial self-awareness, according to Arlene Lev, therapist and author of *Transgender Emergence*, is one of "reaching out."[2] This is when the transperson will begin to share information with those who have been in similar situations or those who may be able to provide some understanding.

COMING OUT TO FAMILY AND CLOSE FRIENDS

An adult who reveals that he or she is transgender can encounter a wide range of reactions from family and close friends. Parents, siblings, spouses, children, loved ones, and friends connected to a transperson may feel as if they have no concept of what it would be like to be in the transperson's shoes. Most people go through a lifetime without so much as thinking about what their gender means to them. When something as fundamental as gender is called into question by a friend or a loved one, many people feel as if the rug has been pulled out from underneath them.

Parents of Trans Adults

No matter how old we get, our parents will always view us as their child. And no matter whether someone is a teenager or is middle aged, coming out can cause family turmoil. Many parents wonder what went wrong in the rearing of their child; they may blame themselves or the other parent. Some parents may have thought that their child was gay, lesbian, or bisexual, but have never considered the possibility of transgenderism. Because many people are uneducated about the subject, they may feel blindsided by such a revelation.

Transpeople come out to their parents in many different ways. Some choose to do it in person, on the phone, via e-mail, by letter, or through a third party. There are certain advantages and disadvantages to using each of these methods. It comes down to personal preference.

Sometimes parents do not initially think about the struggle their child has gone through, but sometimes it is all they can think about. Parents may react with anger and hostility, feeling a combination of betrayal and a sense of loss. It is difficult for a parent who has raised a child to think that he or she could have missed the signs pointing toward something as significant as transgenderism. However, we know that gender transition is the furthest thing from most people's minds, and our minds can do incredible things to keep us from realizing our biggest fears. For example, it is easy, and quite common, for parents to pass off their "daughter's" lifelong masculinity as an extended phase of tomboyishness rather than face the fact that they have actually always had a son rather than a daughter.

One common reaction of parents is to tell their child (even if that child is forty) that he or she is being selfish and not thinking about the effect that coming out might have on the larger family. What these parents might not understand is how torn their child has likely been over whether gender transition would hurt the family and that their child has already delayed coming out as long as possible. Another prevalent parental reaction is guilt for the years of pain and inner turmoil that the child, now an adult, has gone through. There may be guilt surrounding the fact that parents did not notice or address their child's anguish. In many cases, although there may have been signs of gender variance throughout someone's childhood, nothing could have been done to bring the issue to light beforehand. As we have learned, the symptoms are not as concrete and easy to see as one might think.

Parents need a lot of time to adjust to the news of their child, however old, coming out as trans. Most parents feel a sense of loss in the process. A mother of a transwoman, for example, might feel as if she has lost her son. In spite of the fact that she may be gaining a daughter, that loss is still difficult. This mother might feel guilty about her feelings of loss because she did not actually lose a child. It may be difficult for a parent to talk to others about the situation. In cases where no support is available, everything inevitably becomes more difficult. If the parent does disclose her child's news, she may find that people are unsympathetic, freaked out, or unwilling to believe that the parent isn't to blame for the child's transgenderism. Of course, she may also find a great deal of support, depending on whom she tells.

Every parent has a dream for what his or her child will become and how that will unfold, and coming out as trans can do serious damage to—even kill—that dream. Grief over the loss of this dream must take its course naturally. Internet support groups for parents of transpeople are very popular. As with many other things, only a limited amount of support (though undoubtedly needed) can come from those who have not been through the same process.

When parents do decide to begin disclosing to others outside their inner circle that their child is trans, the way they deliver the news is as important, if not more important, than the news itself. It is common for people to take their cues on how to respond from the bearer of the news. If a parent hesitantly tells another person that her child just came out as trans and the parent is visibly upset, the person receiving the news will probably share those feelings. On the other hand, if the parent delivers the news that "Emma is transgender; he is now going by Dan, and he is doing great," the receiver of the news will likely react with acceptance, at least in that moment. After all, the parent in the latter case is not inviting an opinion or any commentary on the subject. Whether or not the person receiving the news is shocked by it, it is clear that the parent in this example feels confident in disclosing this information.

Unfortunately, some parents never adjust. Adolescents and young adults still dependent on parents may face rejection not only emotionally, but also in the form of loss of financial support and possibly housing. Adults at any stage of life may lose their parents' support after coming out. Needless to say, the devastating effects of such rejection are far reaching.

Siblings

Siblings often have a difficult time with the coming-out process. Siblings who are children or adolescents will undoubtedly face a period of time in which they receive less attention from parents and other family members who may be distracted by, and possibly distraught over, what another child has revealed.

Siblings of transmen may feel a significant loss of the sister they once had. Many brothers, older ones especially, feel that they ought to be their sister's protector, looking out for her well-being. When this sister transitions to become a brother, it can be difficult for the male sibling to relate to this new identity. This is especially true of brothers who have watched their only sister transition to become a man. Sisters of transmen may be losing a confidant or a same-sex role model. Similarly, siblings of transwomen often struggle with the fact that their brother is now their sister and they must deal with all the consequences of that change.

Siblings sometimes have more intimate relationships with each other than they do with their parents.[3] Siblings share a relationship with one another that is unique, whether positive or negative. Redefining this lifelong relationship when one sibling transitions can be a major challenge.

Friends

With news this big, it is easy to imagine good friends getting caught off guard. Though some initially react negatively and slowly become supportive over time, the opposite can occur. Some people will react positively or neutrally in the moment and then, once they sit down to think about the news, they become uncomfortable and withdraw from their trans friend.

Friends experience many of the same feelings of loss that family members do. There is, almost without exception, an adjustment period. If two men have been close friends and one of them reveals that she is in fact a transwoman, it may be difficult for the friend to feel that he can continue to relate to his trans friend in the same way that he always has.

Likewise, a woman whose close "girlfriend" reveals that he is a transman may have obstacles to overcome in the relationship.

Many friends of transpeople feel betrayed during the coming-out process. They might say, "We told each other everything; how could you keep such an instrumental part of your life from me?" As we know, often the transperson has been unaware of his or her own situation. Still, it may be difficult to convince a close friend that this is the case. Some transpeople might have deliberately kept their secret from even their closest friends because of fear of losing them. It is a common saying that if one loses a friend over something like gender transition, then that person was not a true friend in the first place. While this may sound sensible, it is always difficult to lose a friend. Sometimes the loss may not be permanent, but many transpeople have to prepare themselves for at least some permanent losses.

A transperson must face his or her family, friends, coworkers, and every acquaintance down to the person who works at the local convenience store. That could number in the hundreds, even thousands, of people. To have to come out to each and every one of them is a daunting task, but two things can make this process easier. One is as old as the human race: gossip. It spreads quickly. The other is the Internet, a somewhat more recent phenomenon and an invention that has made spreading news that much easier. Both of these are double-edged swords that can also make life more difficult for a person in transition. We cannot control the way people talk about us, or whom they talk to, or where they choose to make their opinions known. There will always be people who are out to mock others' struggles or who wish to be the first to tell everyone the big news. Nevertheless, many transpeople find e-mail and social networking sites to be a very convenient way to come out. In one simple announcement they can reach everyone from close friends to long-ago acquaintances.

Spouses and Children of Transpeople

For many years, helping professionals advised that a trans individual with a family should leave the family, state, town, and even country of residence to begin a completely new life elsewhere. It was as if trans individuals had the same needs as those who go into the Witness Protection Program. The rationale for this way of thinking was that there would be no chance of the transperson being accepted in his or her home, workplace, or community, so the best option would be to leave and never look back. Now, because of more comprehensive support resources and visibility of the trans community, there is a greater likelihood of being able to stay put. The thought of having to permanently leave one's family, friends, and home is devastating. However, even today, complete rejection is still a reality for many transpeople.

So what happens when a heterosexual couple is seemingly happily married and the husband comes out as a transwoman? Well, a variety of things can happen, from complete acceptance over time to ugly divorces with bitter custody battles. This has to do with the feelings of each partner in the marriage; there is no right or wrong way to deal with transition in this case. Just as each couple deals differently with any major bump in their relationship, each couple deals differently with a newly-out transgender member.

Jennifer Finney Boylan, transgender author and college professor who fathered two sons with her wife prior to her male-to-female transition, wrote a memoir titled *She's Not There*. The following is part of a conversation between Jennifer and her wife (called Grace in the book) just after Jennifer had come out as trans:

> "You can't expect me to feel the way you do about this. I can't imagine what it's like for you, even now. I'm not the one who's trapped in the wrong body, in the wrong life, in the wrong place. At least I didn't used to be. No matter what happens from here on out, I lose." [Grace's] lower lip trembled.
>
> "I'm sorry," I said.
>
> "I know you're sorry," Grace said. "But what can I say to you? You don't want to be the person I married." She shrugged. "I do love you. But this isn't what I signed up for. This isn't what I had in mind, when I spent the last twelve years, building something."
>
> "It was something I built, too," I said.
>
> We both sat there for a long time then, not saying anything.

"For all that," Grace said, "I still believe that being together is better than being apart. I still want to be with you."[4]

Of course, this is an example of a couple who decided to stay together, and that is likely the exception, not the rule. However, it is important to know that it is possible and that it does happen. Because our society is so centered on the gender binary, something that immediately comes to mind with a transitioning partner is: what, then, is the sexual orientation of the wife of this transwoman, or the husband of a transman? And what does that mean for the spouse's sexual orientation when she or he first fell in love with a person who, as it turns out, is actually trans? We touched on this a bit in the last chapter. In the end, some spouses realize that they love the person whom they married, not the perceived gender of the person. Others realize that they can only be romantically happy with someone who identifies as the original sex of their spouse. Still others make a choice based on many factors. It is similar for same-sex couples when one partner transitions to the other gender; the spouse of the transperson may feel as if he or she has been left with an identity crisis.

Just like any situation where two parents are at odds with each other, a parent's transition can take a toll on the children. If one spouse's transition is causing turmoil in the marriage, it will likely cause turmoil in the entire household. The nontransitioning parent may try to convince the children that the transgender parent is wrong or sick. The transitioning parent may try to level with the children without the spouse present, which can be confusing, especially when the parents have opposing viewpoints. Generally speaking, younger children have an easier time taking the news that one of their parents is trans. Most young kids take things at face value; as long as you are the same person inside and can relate to them the way that they like, they can adjust rather quickly. Jennifer Finney Boylan's children call her "Maddy." It is a combination of mommy and daddy that seemed to fit perfectly for their family.[5]

Adolescents can be quite a different story than younger kids. It is not easy for teenagers to take the news of a parent's transgenderism in stride, but it can be worse if the impending transition is kept a secret

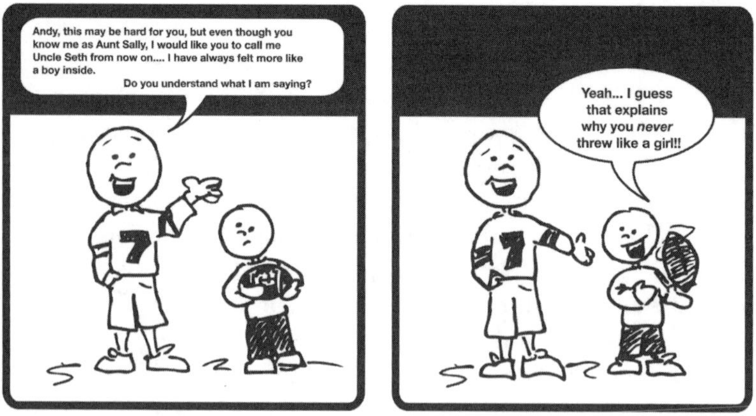

Figure 3.1

Source: © 2010 Jennifer Levo. Text of cartoons by Nicholas M. Teich

from the child.[6] When the news breaks, the teenager must then choose whether or not to tell his or her friends, though in the end, the entire community will likely find out anyway. This can be a frustrating position for someone who is already trying to figure out how to fit in. Many adolescents find that their friends are surprisingly supportive and may even help change their mind about their parent. Some adolescents are understanding of their parent's needs from the beginning and will readily attend family therapy sessions.

Adult children of a transgender parent can react to their parent's coming out in many different ways depending on personal views, the status of the current relationship with the transitioning parent, and so on. The older someone is, the more difficult it is to learn to view such seemingly fixed things as gender in a new light.

COMING OUT IN THE WORKPLACE

People who come out once they are settled into a career generally face fewer obstacles than do people who come out when they are just starting a job. Either way, there is the issue of bosses and coworkers and how they handle the news of their associate. Some coworkers may easily be able to get past the news and treat the transperson the way that person would like to be treated. There may be coworkers who are uncomfortable and upset by the news and thus will withdraw from having conversations with the transperson. Then there will be those coworkers who only think of the transperson as a constant piece of news or gossip, never getting past the initial news.[7]

Oftentimes coworkers will have a chance to see the transition coming. A transwoman may begin to change her daily appearance from male to female by gradually growing out her hair, dressing in more feminine clothing, and even discussing her change in appearance.[8] This may bring the issue to the forefront before an official announcement is made regarding a trans employee's status. This conversation may snowball into an earlier-than-expected announcement to the entire workplace. Depending on the environment, this can be a positive or a negative.

Bathrooms can become a major bone of contention in the workplace. Male employees who knew a coworker as a woman may express discomfort when that coworker, a transman, begins to use the men's room. The same goes for female employees and transwomen. Usually the company or place of business itself must decide how best to handle the situation.

The majority of corporations, businesses, and other workplaces do not specifically protect transgender employees from being fired due to their gender identity. There are no laws regarding this subject in most towns, cities, counties, or states. Therefore, a trans employee faces not only social risk during transition, but risk of losing his or her job as well. This subject is covered in more detail in chapter 7.

TRANSGENDER CHILDREN AND COMING OUT

There can't really be transgender children, can there? Kids can't know for sure how they feel when they're really young, right? Wrong. If you take a controversial subject like transgenderism and add children to the mix, it becomes extremely controversial. The vast majority of adults would be hesitant to believe that a child can make such a serious decision as gender transition. But it is possible.

A mother of natal male and female twins, who goes by the name of Stephanie G., wrote of her struggle to figure out how to support a son who felt that he was always meant to be a daughter:

> Just before first grade began, one hot August night, I was putting [Ryan] to bed and we were saying our prayers. When he ended, he looked at me and said "I'm so mad at God. Every night after I say my prayers, I close my eyes and ask God to make me into a girl, and every morning when I wake up I'm still a boy. God made a mistake mommy and he won't fix it, no matter how hard I wish."
>
> . . . At school, Ryan began to have panic attacks; he had emotional breakdowns daily. He was unable to do his work; he could not concentrate or pay attention.
>
> He would say things to me like "You don't know what it's like to be me" or "Mom, I wish I was dead." . . .
>
> By six years old, Ryan was suicidal. We had to lock the windows upstairs because he threatened, on a regular basis, to jump out and end his life.[9]

Certainly not every case is like this one, but some are, and they warrant attention. Trans children may feel so alien in their world that from the earliest age that they can begin to express themselves (less than two years old), they know that something is seriously wrong. From their perspective, something is wrong with those who keep referring to them as their birth sex. "But I'm a girl," a male-born trans child might say. "Why does everyone keep calling me a boy?"

Though it might seem that anatomy and biology are over a toddler's head, young kids do realize that they have a penis (and shouldn't, in the case of a transgirl) or a vagina (and instead should have a penis, in the case of a transboy). But even before awareness of anatomical differences, children are taught that girls should act a certain way and boys should act a certain way.[10] Transboys labeled female at birth have a bit more leeway in terms of dress and expression (just like their adult counterparts) than transgirls who were labeled male at birth. It is common to see tomboys, but people tend to be less comfortable when they see boys becoming interested in typical "girl stuff." I once spoke to a parent who said that her young son's teacher told her she shouldn't worry if her son wanted to play with dolls and pink toys because the teacher's uncle had been the same way in childhood and grew up to be a manly construction worker. Although the teacher may have been trying to comfort the mother, her message was clear: "Don't worry, your child won't behave the 'wrong' way forever."

As adults, we do not usually take what a two-, five-, or seven-year-old says quite as seriously as, say, a twenty-year-old. Therefore, many parents realize that their trans child is struggling so gravely only when the child threatens to (or does) mutilate his or her body or even becomes suicidal. Unfortunately there are parents who do not even take their children seriously after such threats or other serious behavioral clues.

Gender identity is thought to be solidified by age six.[11] This does not mean that children absolutely, positively know how they identify by that age. It simply means that their gender identity is there. If it doesn't match up with the sex they were assigned at birth, then that will start to manifest itself in different ways, whether visible or not. As we know, it may take decades to figure out one's gender identity, especially because hiding the fact that one is different, in any way, is something most children and even adults will try to do.

Venessia and Joseph Romero, parents of a nine-year-old transgirl named Josie (born Joseph, a male), each reflected on their experience.

Venessia: For years we knew Josie was different. Doctors diagnosed her with ADHD, depression, anxiety disorder, insomnia, reactive bowel disorder, and I don't even remember what else. She was highly medicated, to the point where I called her a walking pharmacy. She simply didn't have the vocabulary to express herself to us and, more importantly, I didn't know how to listen. When she was six years old she would put on dresses, high-heel shoes, raid my make-up and jewelry, and even refused to get her hair cut anymore. Misinterpreting her, I thought she was a gay boy. We don't have a TV and we were living on an ultraconservative military base in Japan, so I didn't have access to a lot of the information I was needing. Finally, the base pediatrician went out on a limb and quietly suggested I look up *transgenderism* online. I did, and wow, how liberating it was to find there was a real word that fit Josie!

As I grew to understand this really was it, not another misdiagnosis, but the real thing, I allowed Josie to select a few outfits to wear at home. After about two weeks, she just wouldn't leave the house in boy clothes again. This led to petitions circulated at the school, picket lines, people throwing things at us and at our house and cars, trash being left on our doorstep, Josie being thrown off her scooter by teenagers, threats of violence, and shunning. Our world had become a scary place to be. We ended up moving back to the States for our own safety.

Joseph: For the first several months, I denied Josie's transgenderism in every way I knew how. Even when I couldn't deny it anymore, I believed it was a phase she would outgrow, and all I cared about was how soon it would be over with. Joey was gone, and I felt like my world was ruined.

Eventually Venessia dragged me to a photo shoot for Josie. I still didn't give a damn about anything, and I went along in an apathetic way. It was at this photo shoot where Josie dressed up like a princess. The shock of seeing her like that made me pay attention. What I saw was my beloved child looking at me with all this hope and fear in her eyes, desperately needing me to give her a smile of my own approval. I made the connection with her then, for the first time, knowing I had gained a daughter. My baby was in there, but not as the boy I thought I had; she was a vibrant, loving, shy, little girl who was terrified of losing her daddy. After the first few frames both Josie and I were wearing genuine smiles and laughing out loud. I had found love in my heart for my beautiful daughter, and that love grows exponentially every day.[12]

Children who are not labeled as trans but rather have gender expressions and identities that do not conform to the norms for their given sex may be called *gender variant* or *gender nonconforming*. These children face their own set of difficulties. Some people may blame a parent for allowing any gender-variant behavior. Others will be curious. "What's going on with Jennifer?" a friend or family member might ask a parent. "Does she feel like a girl or a boy? Which one? And when are you going to make that decision so that people will know how to refer to her?" Imagine the pressure of those questions when your child seems perfectly content to be gender variant. Somehow the answer "She is what she is right now" doesn't satisfy people the way it should. Tempting though it may be during a time of gender crisis in the household, it can be dangerous (not to mention extremely stressful on parent and child) to try to push a child into transitioning genders simply because adults want to know which gender he or she is. Likewise, it won't work to try to keep a gender-variant child boxed into the societal norms of his or her birth sex. One important thing to keep in mind is that not all gender-variant children grow up to be transgender. In fact, most do not. This is another reason for parents to listen closely to their children and go with the flow, as difficult as that may be.

Parents of young children who come out as trans face a very complicated set of issues when making decisions that affect schooling, friends, community, and their own relationship with the child. Oftentimes parents do not agree on how to handle the rearing of a trans child, which can put a strain on the marriage or partnership. If one parent decides that the only way to see little Josh smile is to let him/her wear a dress when s/he goes out in public, and the other parent is dead set against that, serious problems can arise.

Parents of trans children, if they are listening to their kid, will likely end up bringing the child to some sort of mental health professional. However, there is still no official standard for how to treat transpeople (see chapter 6 for *gender identity disorder*). Each professional is left to decide how to advise parents to proceed. Similarly, before 1973, homosexuality was listed as a mental disorder; parents who believed that their child was not mentally ill tried to visit professionals who had similar opinions, and vice versa for those who did believe that their child was mentally ill.

Statistics on trans children are few and far between. We do not know how children fare when their parents do not acknowledge their severe distress, but one can only imagine that the child will continue to spiral downward. Some trans children are very open about their identities, but some want very much to blend in, understandably. So when they begin living as their "correct" gender, they may stop coming out. For example, if Michael transitions to Michelle and goes to a new school where no one knows her, she may not want anyone to know that she was labeled male at birth. She may want to be stealth, to fit in with the other girls her age, and may even resent anyone that does know her secret. These feelings may or may not change as she gets older.

Now that we know a bit more about coming out, let us embark on some of the many journeys that make up transition.

4

TRANSITION

The Social, the Emotional, and the Medical

Transition is a term that people often refer to as "sex change." We will talk about why that is far from the best term to use. There are several different ways in which transpeople transition, so let us look at them.

SOCIAL TRANSITION

Transitioning socially is often the most difficult part of the journey. Much of social transition entails coming out to people, which we learned about in chapter 3. But for the transperson, social transition means learning to finally live in the world as his or her true self. Transitioning socially can be utterly terrifying, but can also be one of the most rewarding steps of one's life.

During transition, many transwomen experience—for the first time in their lives—what it is like to be treated as a woman. Many transwomen speak of "loss of status," particularly white transwomen who were socialized as white men. Autumn Sandeen, a fifty-year-old navy veteran and transgender woman, talks about her initial experiences at the Department of Veterans Affairs (VA) after transitioning:

> I noted for the first time that the heterosexual women were noticing me—about three or four of them had an angry or jealous look in their eyes because I looked like an attractive, older woman . . . [and] the men were flirting with me. It was really strange. First time in my life that happened.
>
> But then, I chose to be out as trans . . . and these fairly decent folk began calling me "he" because that's how they now perceived me. That always seems a bit painful.[1]

Autumn's story is unfortunately typical of those who socially transition and subsequently come out as transgender to people who did not already know. People tend to take others at face value. If a transwoman looks, acts, and walks like a woman, so to speak, then there is no reason to doubt that she has always been female. But once Autumn revealed her transgender status, some people felt that they must delegitimize her gender identity by using male pronouns—even though up until a moment before she came out they had no idea that Autumn "used to be male." Oftentimes this stems from embarrassment. If you ask people in general if they think they would always be able to identify a transgender person, they would likely say yes. This is because the general perception of a transgender person is a man in a dress. When that perception is challenged, as it was in Autumn's case, people can feel duped. But Autumn is not duping anyone. She is only living her life and is coming out because she thinks it is important to be a role model for others.

Now let's look at an example from transman Matt Kailey, author of *Just Add Hormones: An Insider's Guide to the Transsexual Experience*. Labeled female at birth, Matt began his social transition in his thirties. Although he had felt like a man for his entire life, it took courage and time to tell people to use the pronouns "he" and "him" instead of "she" and "her." Matt experienced a rebirth of sorts during his transition. He had this to say about being seen as a man for the first time:

> I have found that people are not as friendly to me as they were when I was a woman. I think this has to do with an expectation that men are not as friendly as women in general. When I was a woman, they expected me to be cordial, and so they approached me openly and cheerfully. Because I'm a man now, the expectation is that I will not be as friendly, so other people are not as pleasant to me as they used to be. I have also noticed that salesclerks are not as eager to offer help as they were when I was a woman—this goes for both male and female salesclerks. I think people assume that men can figure things out for themselves, and they assume that women will need help. This, in my opinion, is based on society's sexist view of women as more helpless and less capable than men.[2]

Kailey agrees that "male privilege is alive and well," but his experiences show us that being perceived as a man has another side to it that some would consider unprivileged.

Many transmen talk about feeling invisible. This is because, as noted before, the general perception of a transgender person is on the male-to-female spectrum rather than the female-to-male spectrum. Transmen are often assumed to be biological males and are not given a second thought because many people are not aware that female-to-male transpeople exist. This can be both a pro and a con.

Just as transwomen can experience a loss of status, transmen can experience what it feels like to be treated as a man in our society. (Of course, other factors such as race and ethnicity also play into how people are treated.) This may sound like a promotion of sorts for the transman, but as Matt's story tells us, it is not always that way. Transmen who identify as feminists can feel highly conflicted about the new way in which they are being seen in the world. And just as our MTF example Autumn experienced, once a transwoman reveals her identity, she is subject to ridicule and being called "he."

It doesn't seem fair to say that either transmen or transwomen have it easier. However, one important piece of social transition, appearance, is almost universally more difficult for transwomen, for a number of reasons. First, there are lots of nontransgender women who wear baseball caps or polo shirts or baggy jeans, or any number of other typically masculine styles of clothing. That was not always the case, but in recent decades it has become socially acceptable for women to dress in a masculine manner (to a point). This is true of young girls especially, who may be labeled as tomboys if they like to wear hats and never like to wear skirts or dresses. But for boys and men, the opposite does not hold true. It has never been socially acceptable for men to wear women's clothes in public. So, growing up as boys, transwomen are held to a certain, very strict standard of gender expression. Additionally, many transwomen have a naturally prominent jaw line and brow, large hands, and a tall stature. This can cause major difficulty when trying not to stand out. While transmen often have softer, smaller features and a shorter stature than most men, they still tend to be able to blend in more easily than transwomen. The choice to use or not use hormones plays a big part in this, as well.

HORMONAL TRANSITION

Many transpeople elect to take synthetic hormones, but some do not. For those who do, the physical and emotional changes are immense.

Male-to-Female Hormonal Regimen

For transwomen, taking hormones is a two-step process. Because testosterone, the main male hormone, is so powerful, transwomen need to take androgen suppressants in addition to female hormones. Without going into too much medical detail, androgen suppressants lessen the effects of male hormones. Testosterone is the most powerful of the male hormones. To help feminize a biological male, it is very important to suppress production of testosterone. The other step MTFs frequently take is the administration of estrogen, which is the chief hormone at work in biological females. Transwomen generally take estrogen in pill form, as a skin patch, or via injection.[3] Transwomen usually take estrogen as a lifelong (or at least long-term) treatment.

So what do androgen suppressants and estrogens do to feminize a natal male? They do several things. Transwomen go through some of the same things that girls entering puberty do, as both groups are experiencing a surge of estrogen for the first time. The following is not an exhaustive list of physical effects for MTF hormone treatment, but these are some of the most commonly occurring:

1. Breast tissue increases. Transwomen will not get very large breasts from hormone treatment alone, but their breast tissue will grow steadily for the first few years on estrogen. Those who wish to increase breast size can opt for surgery after they have been on estrogen for a while.
2. Estrogen decreases body hair growth in most places, but facial hair in biological males is often resistant to estrogen.[4] Many transwomen must go through the costly, time-consuming, and painful process of electrolysis to keep facial hair from returning. Estrogen helps prevent baldness in biological males, but it will not necessarily provide regrowth in bald spots already present.[5]
3. Estrogen helps to redistribute body fat from a male pattern into a more female pattern (curvier shape; fat shifts from the abdomen to the thighs, hips, and buttocks). Additionally, transwomen often experience a decrease in muscle mass and in the ability to build muscle.
4. The combination of androgen suppressants and introduction of estrogen will likely cause a decrease in libido and/or amount of ejaculate,[6] as well as cause changes in sperm production. This can adversely affect fertility.
5. Transwomen often experience softer skin texture with the help of the female hormone regimen.

Estrogen treatments cannot alter the voice of a biological male who has already been through puberty. Many transwomen take voice lessons or hire speech coaches to learn and practice feminine inflection and tone of voice.

In addition to these many physical changes, hormones also have emotional effects, which vary from person to person. It is difficult to discern which emotional changes are caused by the hormones themselves and which result from the transwoman feeling more psychologically complete simply because she has taken the step to begin medical transition. One common psychological effect of the hormone regimen is that transwomen are able to express emotions more easily than they were before taking estrogen.[7]

Many of the effects of estrogen treatment are reversible if the treatment is stopped and the body is again allowed to make testosterone. Breast tissue growth is generally not reversible. Fertility changes may or may not be reversible.[8]

Female-to-Male Hormonal Regimen

Unlike their male-to-female counterparts, transmen do not have to take any estrogen-suppressing substances as part of their hormone treatments. Testosterone (called simply T in the FTM community) is a powerful hormone. The raising of testosterone levels in a transman overpowers existing estrogen levels. The goal is to get testosterone levels within the normal range of a biological male.[9] T is most often injected into the thigh or buttocks once every week to two weeks by a medical professional, the patient himself, or a friend or loved one. These injections can cause peaks and valleys in testosterone levels that may produce slight adverse affects for some transmen. Skin patches and topical gel are available as an alternative. These methods generally ensure a steadier level of the hormone than injections do.[10]

Transmen taking male hormones experience some of the same things that boys in puberty do because of the similar surge in testosterone. The following is, again, not an exhaustive list of side effects of FTM hormone treatment, but are some of the most commonly occurring:

1. Menstruation ceases. This is often one of the most important things that testosterone does to a transman. Having a monthly period can be devastating when a person identifies as a man. If this does not happen within about six months, a physician may adjust dosage levels until the desired effects take place.

2. Testosterone increases body hair and facial hair growth, which may take several years. Along with the growth of body and facial hair comes the possibility of male-pattern baldness. Just as it does in biological males, this depends on a person's genes. Facial hair and possible baldness are what enable some transmen to pass so well and blend in.
3. Hormone therapy in transmen changes the pitch of the voice, unlike hormones for transwomen. Generally the voice lowers to within the range of a biological male's voice, though not in every case.
4. Transmen taking testosterone will likely experience a higher libido than they did before taking the hormones.[11]
5. Unlike transwomen, who experience breast growth with hormone therapy, transmen's breast tissue does not normally decrease because of testosterone. Because of this, many transmen prefer to bind their chests with a device or tightly layered clothing that makes the breasts much less visible. The long-term effects of binding can include breathing problems and back pain.[12] Many FTMs eventually opt for *top surgery* (explained in the next section).
6. Skin texture may feel coarser with the use of testosterone.
7. Body fat will redistribute from a female pattern to a male pattern (fat shifts from the thighs, hips, and buttocks to the abdomen).
8. Transmen often experience increase in lean muscle mass, making the total body weight higher.[13]
9. Clitoral enlargement is another effect of testosterone use in transmen. The clitoral length ends up in the range of about 3.5–6.0 cm (1.4–2.4 inches) when stretched.[14]
10. Acne and oily skin is a common side effect of testosterone therapy, at least in the beginning. As mentioned before, the first years of testosterone use can be comparable to puberty in biological males.
11. Testosterone use may prevent transmen from being able to conceive and carry a child.

Like transwomen taking female hormones, transmen taking testosterone also experience emotional effects that vary depending on certain personal factors. Some transmen may feel that expressing emotions (crying, for instance) is more difficult than it was prior to beginning testosterone.

Many of the effects of testosterone are reversible if treatment is stopped. Those that are not thought to be reversible include voice change, facial hair growth, and male-pattern baldness. It is unknown whether clitoral growth and sterility are reversible and may vary from person to person.[15]

SURGERIES

No matter what type of transgender surgery a person gets, it always takes an immense financial commitment. Health insurance covers transgender surgeries in very few cases. Since most people pay out of pocket, the costs can be astronomical. Because of this, many transpeople never have surgery. Some people have fewer surgeries than they would like because of the high prices. Still other transpeople elect not to have surgery because they simply do not want to.

In recent years there has been a call to revise the wording that describes transgender surgery. For a long time, and still in many places today, people refer to some transgender surgery as "sex change" surgery. Later on came the less-harsh-sounding "sex reassignment surgery," or *SRS*. SRS is still used commonly today. Because people began to learn about the differences between sex and gender, the more specific term "genital reassignment/reconstruction surgery," or *GRS*, came into use. GRS can also refer to *gender reassignment surgery*, which is similar to sex reassignment surgery. Today, more and more people are realizing that surgery for transpeople is not a gender "reassignment" but rather an affirmation of the gender that a person has always been. *Gender-affirming surgery* seems to be the most accurate reflection of this, and for the purposes of this book, I will use it. However, I do not believe that people are using its acronym!

The following are some descriptions of different surgeries that are offered to the transgender population. These are some of the most common, but this is by no means a complete list.

In Male-to-Female Transpeople

Breast Augmentation Surgery (Mammoplasty)

If given hormones, MTFs may experience breast growth. However, this growth is often not satisfactory because it does not usually reach the full breast development of an adult natal female. Thus some transwomen opt for breast augmentation surgery. This procedure is not unlike breast augmentation surgery, or breast enlargement, for non-trans women.

Genital Surgery

Genital surgery for transwomen generally involves a *vaginoplasty* (creation of a vagina out of the penis) and an *orchiectomy* (removal of the testicles). In most cases the penile skin is essentially turned inside out to form the lining of the new vagina.[16] The sensitive tip of the penis is used to form the new clitoris. The scrotal sac skin is then used to form the labia majora.[17] There are other techniques for performing this surgery, but this seems to be the most well-regarded one.

Facial Feminization Surgery

Because natal males generally have more angular and prominent facial features than natal females, some transwomen take steps to make their face appear more feminine. A transwoman may undergo one or more of the following procedures.

One component of facial feminization surgery is recontouring of the forehead. A female's brow is higher than a male's and the distance between the brow and the hairline is shorter in females.[18] Transwomen also often undertake a reshaping of the nose to a smaller and more feminine appearance. Many transwomen have their chins reshaped to look more feminine. This can include reshaping the jaw line, depending on how severe and masculine-looking the angle is. Cheek implants are also a component of facial feminization surgery for some people. Another common procedure is reduction of the Adam's apple, also known as *trachea shave* or *chondrolaryngoplasty*.[19]

In Female-to-Male Transpeople

Chest Surgery or Top Surgery

Many FTMs will go through a surgical procedure that reconstructs the chest to look like a natal male's chest. Depending on breast size of the patient, there are different methods of doing the surgery. Some people, mainly those who have larger breasts, will have a *double-incision mastectomy* with free nipple grafts. In this procedure, to achieve a male-looking result, the nipples often must be resized, reshaped, and placed in the proper masculine position on the chest. (This is different from a mastectomy that a breast cancer patient might undergo because of the male chest reconstruction that follows the mastectomy.) Those with smaller breasts may have *periareolar*, or *keyhole surgery*, which uses liposuction and generally does not require repositioning of the nipples. Both procedures are considered major surgery, although many patients are discharged from the hospital or surgery center without having to stay overnight.

Bottom Surgery or Lower Surgery

This surgery is less common for FTMs than is top surgery. There are two well-known types of bottom surgery and several others as well. We will focus on a brief description of two types of bottom surgery: *metoidioplasty* and *phalloplasty*.

Metoidioplasty can be done in transmen who are taking testosterone. This procedure consists of releasing the clitoris, which has been sufficiently enlarged by testosterone, so that it extends out farther. At that point it will resemble a small penis. The urethra can be extended and rerouted through the new penis so that urinating in a standing position is possible. Some transmen elect to have the vagina permanently closed and to have a scrotum formed out of existing tissue. Testicular implants are then added to the scrotum.[20]

During phalloplasty, a penis is constructed using skin from another site on the body (the abdomen or forearm, for example). If the skin donor site is the forearm, a penis is created with a "tube-in-tube" technique while the skin is still attached to the arm.[21] It is then moved to the pubic area. Often a phalloplasty is accompanied by the closing of the vagina, extension of the urethra, and creation of a scrotum.[22] A complete phalloplasty usually includes multiple surgeries. Nerves are connected so that the patient's new penis will be sensate, although there is no guarantee that this will be successful, and the results will not be felt immediately in any case. Testicular implants and an erectile prosthesis can be added after the penis regains sensation, which usually takes at least a year.[23] The penis is usually comparable in size to that of a biological male.

Historically, many transmen who have had phalloplasty have not been satisfied with the results. Doctors continue to make improvements to this surgery, but many surgeons in the United States choose not to perform it because of the high risk of complications (severe scarring or fistulas for example), the significant risk of never regaining sensation in the penis or donor sites, and the chance that the result will not be aesthetically pleasing. However, some transmen are satisfied with their results and would choose to do it again if given the choice.

Hysterectomy

Some transmen opt to have their uterus removed, a procedure commonly known as *hysterectomy*. It may or may not be accompanied by removal of the cervix, ovaries, and fallopian tubes. Some FTMs undergo removal of the ovaries alone, which is known as an *oophorectomy*. Many transmen feel that these parts of them are foreign and simply do not belong in their body. Others want to produce as little estrogen as possible. Still others may have the procedure to prevent having annual visits to a gynecologist, which can be a traumatic experience for a transman. There is debate among medical professionals about the long-term effects of testosterone on the FTM reproductive system, and some doctors recommend a hysterectomy and/or oophorectomy as a prophylactic measure.

DOES A PERSON NEED "PERMISSION" TO HAVE SURGERY OR BEGIN HORMONES?

The answer: most of the time. The Harry Benjamin International Gender Dysphoria Association was the first professional group to form and write up standards on how to go about treating trans patients. This association has since been renamed the World Professional Association for Transgender Health (WPATH). However, the official *Standards of Care for the Health of Transsexual, Transgender, and Gender Nonconforming People* are still commonly called the Harry Benjamin Standards of Care. We will learn more about Harry Benjamin in chapter 5. The Standards of Care were written mainly for medical and mental health professionals and are currently in their seventh version (released in September 2011) since the first printing in 1979.[24] The Standards of Care are not binding by law; in fact they are self-described as adjustable guidelines, but they are the closest thing to a universal standard that exists for trans health care.

We are going to look at a few important components of the Standards of Care but will not cover every detail of the lengthy document, including a new section on the treatment of trans children and adolescents. The purpose is to give you a general idea of the usual process for prescribing hormones or allowing surgery for trans adults. See the WPATH resource in appendix B to learn how to get a full copy of the Standards of Care.

The eligibility criteria for adults to begin hormone therapy or have top surgery for FTMs or breast augmentation surgery for MTFs include

1. Persistent, well-documented gender dysphoria;
2. Capacity to make a fully informed decision and to consent for treatment;
3. Age of majority in a given country (if younger, follow the *Standards of Care* outlined in section VI ["Assessment and Treatment of Children and Adolescents with Gender Dysphoria"]);
4. If significant medical or mental health concerns are present, they must be reasonably well-controlled.[25]

Eligibility for a hysterectomy and/or removal of ovaries (for FTMs) or removal of testicles (for MTFs) includes the above criteria plus "12 continuous months of hormone therapy as appropriate to the patient's gender goals (unless the patient has a medical contraindication or is otherwise unable or unwilling to take hormones)."[26] Eligibility for most other genital surgery includes all of the above criteria plus "12 continuous months of living in a gender role that is congruent with their gender identity."[27]

Adults getting hormone therapy need to obtain a letter of support or documentation from a health professional. This can be a mental health professional or another health care provider who has training in the area of assessing people with gender dysphoria. The Standards of Care recommend that the letter or documentation include the following:

1. The client's general identifying characteristics;
2. Results of the client's psychosocial assessment, including any diagnoses;
3. The duration of the referring health professional's relationship with the client, including the type of evaluation and therapy or counseling to date;
4. An explanation that the criteria for hormone therapy have been met, and a brief description of the clinical rationale for supporting the client's request for hormone therapy;
5. A statement about the fact that informed consent has been obtained from the patient;
6. A statement that the referring health professional is available for coordination of care and welcomes a phone call to establish this.[28]

For FTM top surgery or MTF breast augmentation surgery, a mental health professional must make a referral, usually in the form of a letter. For any genital surgeries or hysterectomy, two separate letters are needed from two different mental health professionals (or two professionals may both sign the same letter). Alternatively, a "multidisciplinary specialty team" may document its assessment in the person's chart. The criteria for the letter or assessment for any surgery is the same as it is for hormones except that in number four the word "surgery" replaces the words "hormone therapy."[29]

The Standards of Care state that there is no requirement for psychotherapy in order to begin hormones or surgery outside of an assessment as described above. However, the Standards of Care does give guidelines for those mental health professionals who are engaged in psychotherapy with transgender clients.[30]

CHANGING GENDER OR SEX LEGALLY

How do transpeople legally change their gender or sex marker? Typically, each document such as a birth certificate, passport, driver's license, Social Security card, health insurance card, and so on, must be changed one at a time. Each state has different regulations about what is required to change a sex marker on a driver's license; each city or state has its own rules for birth certificates; each insurance company has its own requirements, and so on.

Many states will enable someone to change the sex on his or her driver's license or birth certificate with a surgeon's letter stating that the person has undergone gender-affirming surgery. However, before this can happen, obviously one must have had surgery. And as we have learned, surgery is not what makes someone trans. Some states have come to understand this concept and will change a sex marker with a letter from a mental health professional stating how the transperson identifies his or her gender, regardless of hormonal or other medical intervention. Each agency within the federal government also has its own regulations (Social Security, passports, etc.). Changing gender on a passport used to be touch-and-go, but as of June 2010 the U.S. Department of State changed the law: "When a passport applicant presents a certification from an attending medical physician that the applicant has undergone appropriate clinical treatment for gender transition, the passport will reflect the new gender."[31] This was a big victory for transpeople because "clinical treatment" does not specify surgery; it can also mean psychotherapy.

Name Change

Official documentation is necessary to change one's name on legal documents as well as on everything from employer or school documentation to credit cards. Name changes operate independently of gender or sex change for documentation. In most cases, one can be changed without changing the other. Name changes occur at different times for different people. Some transpeople may choose to legally change their name as soon as possible while others may never legally change it. Name choices are deeply personal decisions. Some people include family members in the decision and others do not. Some people change last names and others keep theirs. There is no single rule on a transperson's name. Legal name change normally goes through the local (usually county) court and is approved by a judge. Some jurisdictions require printing the name change announcement in a local newspaper.

Figure 4.1

Source: © 2010 Jennifer Levo. Text of cartoons by Nicholas M. Teich

TRANSITION IN CHILDREN

Transition for children is quite a bit different than it is for adults. In prepubertal children, secondary sex characteristics such as breasts and facial hair are not yet present. It is therefore easier for a child to look like either sex, depending on hair length and clothing choice. In recent years, parents with transgender children have had more options for their kids' care.

As we know, trans youth are often in emotional dire straits before receiving the attention they need. Once puberty is allowed to take its course, trans children must endure what can be sheer terror: experiencing the development of secondary sex characteristics of their natal sex. However, if a child takes puberty-inhibiting medication (it's exactly what it sounds like), the development of these secondary sex characteristics is put on hold until the child and parents are able to come to a decision on how to proceed with transition into adulthood. The family and physician of a transgender child can decide the best course of action up to several years after the introduction of puberty-inhibiting medication. If the child and parents decide that transition is not the right path, then the child can revert back to living as his or her natal sex simply by stopping the medication. When the medication is discontinued, puberty of the biological sex will resume as normal.[32] However, it is extremely rare that such a decision is made.

More commonly, the child and parents decide to continue with transition into adulthood and at some point the child begins to take the hormones of the gender he or she identifies as, thus entering puberty in that gender. For instance, if a male-to-female trans child, after several years on puberty inhibitors, decides that she indeed identifies as a woman and wants to move forward, she will be put on estrogen and will develop normally like any female child going through puberty (with the exception of genitalia and internal organs). The decision about genital surgery is usually made at age eighteen or older, but there are some exceptions for younger children if they have parental permission and a go-ahead from mental health and medical professionals.[33] It is very important to keep in mind that none of the aforementioned decisions are ones that parents, children, or professionals take lightly.

Puberty-inhibiting medication is usually only available to those who can afford its steep price, and it is useful only for youth who are aware of their gender incongruence before puberty hits full force. Like other transgender-related medications and procedures, most health insurance companies deem puberty inhibitors elective and therefore unnecessary (though that is far from the case). A growing number of trans youth are receiving help with puberty-inhibiting medication, but those who cannot afford it, those who have unsupportive parents, and those who have gone through puberty already often end up in a tough spot. The wait can be long and painful for a child who is already going through puberty and must wait to medically transition until he or she is sixteen or eighteen.

5

THE HISTORY OF TRANSGENDERISM AND ITS EVOLUTION OVER TIME

DR. HARRY BENJAMIN: THE "FATHER OF TRANSSEXUALISM"

Endocrinologist Harry Benjamin is known as the "founding father of contemporary western transsexualism."[1] Born in Germany but living most of his professional life in New York, he treated some 1,500 trans patients over the span of his career from the time of World War I until the mid-1970s.[2] One of his first trans patients was referred to him by Dr. Alfred Kinsey, the famous sexologist and professor at Indiana University.[3]

Dr. Magnus Hirschfeld, a German doctor who worked with Benjamin beginning early in his career, was among the first to talk about the difference between being a feminine gay man and a transwoman (though he did not use this terminology).[4] Many people conflated the two terms, as they still do now. Benjamin went on to expand on Hirschfeld's work.

Benjamin believed that transpeople suffered from a medical, rather than a psychological, condition. Because of this, he was at odds with most psychiatrists of the day, many of whom diagnosed transpeople (transwomen especially) with being delusional or having schizophrenia.[5] Benjamin brought legitimacy to the feeling of being born or living in the wrong body.[6] In 1966, his book *The Transsexual Phenomenon,* the first of its kind, was published. Many people who might have used the Internet to find help and resources, had it been available to them, instead wrote to Dr. Benjamin and a handful of other doctors. Benjamin was seen as an important advocate for transpeople, and not only in the medical sense.[7] In response to one of the many heart-wrenching letters he received from young patients seeking his advice, Benjamin wrote words that opened up possibilities to the youngster with the following: "You have your whole life ahead of you. Something can and will be done for you. Just be patient and eventually you will lead a happier life than you do now."[8]

The Harry Benjamin International Gender Dysphoria Association (now called the World Professional Association of Transgender Health, or WPATH) was named in Benjamin's honor in 1978. WPATH oversees the *International Journal of Transgenderism,* a scholarly journal, and has written and maintained the Standards of Care for trans patients outlined in chapter 4. Dr. Benjamin died in 1986 at the age of 101 with his faculties still very much intact.[9]

CHRISTINE JORGENSEN AND AMERICA'S INTRODUCTION TO TRANSPEOPLE

George Jorgensen was labeled male at birth and served as a soldier in the U.S. Army during World War II. Upon returning to the States, Jorgensen transitioned from George to Christine, becoming America's first well-publicized transperson. As one can imagine, the news of her transition was not met with immediate acceptance and respect. But once the public learned more about Jorgensen, they began to understand that real transpeople existed.

Shortly after returning home from war, Jorgensen began to read books at the library about the power of hormones over masculinity and femininity. In her autobiography, she said, "I didn't know how my own case might be related to these ideas but at that moment it seemed possible to me that I was holding salvation in my hands: the science of body chemistry. Even then, I think I knew that Providence had intervened again and opened a door on a new and shining vista."[10]

Jorgensen first met Dr. Harry Benjamin after she had already begun taking female hormones under the care of a different endocrinologist.[11] Benjamin would later write the introduction to her 1967 autobiography, in which he said: "Her success as a woman is no longer in doubt."[12] Her genital surgery was performed in 1952 by transgender surgical pioneer Dr. Paul Fogh-Andersen of Denmark.[13]

Jorgensen's autobiography was a way for her to quell the curiosity and near hysteria that the story of her transition created to America. Newspapers announced Jorgensen's story with such headlines as "Ex GI Becomes Blonde Beauty[14]" and "Bronx 'Boy' Is Now a Girl."[15]

Doctors who worked with trans patients after World War II in what can be called the "Jorgensen era" had lower status in their profession and little access to research money earmarked for disease. Those who advocated sex reassignment/gender affirming surgery could not expect support from other doctors, hospitals, the American Medical Association, or the public agencies and private foundations that provided money for research. In fact, both inside and outside the United States the controversy surrounding transsexuality could hurt their professional standing.[16]

Jorgensen's coming out was pivotal on many fronts, but perhaps her most important contribution to the world was proving that transgenderism was a real issue separate from homosexuality and cross-dressing.[17]

THE REIMER CASE AND THE FIGHT OVER NATURE VERSUS NURTURE

We learned a great deal about nature versus nurture from the infamous story of Canadian David Reimer. He was born Bruce Reimer in 1965, a healthy male with an identical twin brother, Brian. In infancy he endured a botched circumcision that left him without a penis. His parents, Janet and Ron Reimer, were at a loss for what to do until they were referred to Dr. John Money, a psychologist at Johns Hopkins University in Baltimore. Together with Money, the Reimers decided it would be easiest to raise Bruce as a girl named Brenda and keep the child's past a secret from her. At age fourteen, Brenda Reimer learned the truth and immediately reverted to living as a boy, which he had always felt he was. Reimer changed his name to David. He later married, was the father to three stepchildren, and ultimately separated from his wife.[18] He committed suicide in 2004 at age thirty-eight by shooting himself in the head with a shotgun.[19] In an interview in 2000, Reimer proclaimed: "You don't wake up one morning deciding if you're a boy or a girl. You just know."[20]

David had a very troubled childhood as Brenda. Dr. Money and the Reimers agreed that Brenda and Brian would make annual visits to Baltimore to see Money. Under Money's supervision, Brenda had plastic surgery to construct a vulva. Money remained adamant that the Reimers keep Brenda's past a secret from everyone.

Money theorized that parents could raise a child to be whatever gender the parents wanted regardless of the child's birth sex or core gender identity.[21] When the Reimers came along, he saw a perfect opportunity to begin documenting an experiment that he thought would prove his case, and Brenda and Brian were the ideal subjects. Obviously, his theory was refuted by the tragic unfolding of events in the Reimer family. Still, Money defended his actions as well as his theory about nurture and gender until his death in 2006 at age eighty-four.

In John Colapinto's book *As Nature Made Him: The Boy Who Was Raised as a Girl*, Janet Reimer recalls an incident after giving Brenda a dress that she had made: "She was ripping at it, trying to tear it off. I remember thinking, Oh my God, she knows she's a boy and doesn't want girls' clothing. She doesn't want to be a girl. But then I thought, Well, maybe I can *teach* her to want to be a girl."[22]

During a session between Brenda and Dr. Money in 1978, Money brought in a transwoman who had gone through a full vaginoplasty to talk to Brenda about it. This was precisely the type of surgery Money was pushing Brenda to have at the time. After the session, Brenda told her parents that she would kill herself if she ever had to see Money again.[23] In the 2000 interview, Reimer said, "I was scared to death. I figured, you know, I was perfectly fine. . . . What do I need surgery for? I thought deep down inside that if I went through this surgery, it would change me somehow."[24]

In the early 1990s, Dr. Milton Diamond, an opponent of many of Money's theories, decided that he wanted to revisit the Reimer case. He convinced David to meet with him. David saw him as genuine and caring and agreed to work with him. Diamond got in touch with the psychiatrist who oversaw David's childhood psychiatric visits in Canada (when he was known as Brenda). In 1994, after hearing David's story and spending some time with him, Diamond wrote an article concluding from the Reimer case that gender identity is inborn. He said that although nurture has an impact on the way a child acts, nature is what is responsible for forming a core sense of gender identity.[25] Diamond is still actively researching gender and sexuality.

Some of Reimer's last words in that 2000 interview reveal a tortured soul. "If you're not going to take my word as gospel, because I've lived through it, who else are you going to listen to? . . . Is it going to take somebody to wind up killing themselves—shooting themselves in the head—for people to listen?"[26]

Prior to David's eventual suicide in 2004, his twin brother Brian overdosed on antidepressants in 2002 and died. In following two years, David's marriage began to fail, and he made a poor investment with a large sum of money, lost his job, and continued to deal with the terror that was his childhood. These events (though mainly his struggle with his childhood) all led up to his death.[27] The Reimer case, sometimes called the John/Joan case, is still cited today in the nature-nurture debate.

OTHER TWENTIETH-CENTURY PIONEERS IN THE TRANS MOVEMENT

Many people share responsibility for helping the trans movement along. This is simply a sample of the great number of people, some famous and some nameless, who promoted the change that has occurred over the past century. Many of them did not set out to do this, but rather looked to help normalize transgenderism.

One of the first patients to undergo successful genital reassignment (gender-affirming) surgery was male-to-female transperson Dora Richter. The surgery was set up by Magnus Hirschfeld in Germany in 1931.[28] FTM surgeries began to follow later on in that decade.

. . . . .

Reed Erickson was a transman born in 1917. He became a patient of Harry Benjamin in 1963 and, because Erickson had inherited a very large fortune from his father, he was able to fund Benjamin's book *The Transsexual Phenomenon*.[29] Erickson's story is especially notable because even in the mid-1960s the American medical community appeared skeptical about the existence of transmen. Joanne Meyerowitz writes in *How Sex Changed*: "At the end of the 1960s doctors at UCLA's Gender Identity Research Clinic debated privately whether FTMs even qualified as transsexuals."[30] After his transition, Erickson started several trans-positive foundations including the Erickson Education Foundation. He played a key role in putting transgenderism on the map.

. . . . .

On June 28, 1969, police raided the Stonewall Inn, a gay bar in Manhattan's Greenwich Village neighborhood. The cops mostly went after transwomen and other gender-nonconforming people because they were the easiest targets. These types of raids on GLBT bars were commonplace, and not just in New York. This time the patrons of Stonewall fought back, and chaos ensued. Stonewall became the name of a movement that jump-started organized GLBT rights in America. Most people described the Stonewall Inn as a gay men's bar and credit that evening in June 1969 with the birth of the organized gay rights movement, but transpeople of all types were very much a part of the Stonewall rebellion.

MILESTONES IN AMERICAN TRANSGENDERISM

1886: We'wha, a two-spirit Native American, visits President Cleveland at the White House.[a]

1914: Harry Benjamin opens his own endocrinology practice in New York.[b]

1929: One of the first well-known transwomen worldwide, Christine Jorgensen, is born in the Bronx.

1951: Jorgensen officially begins life as a woman.

1966: Johns Hopkins University opens its Gender Identity Clinic in Baltimore.[c] The same year, baby Bruce Reimer endures a botched circumcision. Soon after, his parents enlist the help of John Money at the Hopkins Clinic and they begin to raise Reimer as a girl.[d]

1969: Riots erupt after gay and transgender people are arrested at New York's Stonewall Inn bar.

1975: Minneapolis becomes the first American city to pass a law protecting gender identity (though it was in a clause titled "Affectional Preference" and thus may have been unclear at the time).[e]

1978: The Harry Benjamin International Gender Dysphoria Association, now known as WPATH, is formed.

1989: Seventy-five-year-old jazz musician Billy Tipton dies and it is revealed that though he lived as a man for fifty-five years, he was actually born female.

1992: Leslie Feinberg publishes a pamphlet titled *Transgender Liberation*. Feinberg uses the word "transgender" to describe all types of gender-variant people.

1993: Transman Brandon Teena is raped and murdered in Nebraska. The 1999 film *Boys Don't Cry* is based on his story.

1999: The first Transgender Day of Remembrance is held in San Francisco as a vigil to those transpeople who have been killed because of their identity.

2002: Transwoman Gwen Araujo is murdered in California, causing outrage in the GLBT community.

2004: The International Olympic Committee officially decides to allow transsexual athletes to compete if they have had genital reassignment surgery and at least two years of hormone therapy.[f] The same year, David Reimer commits suicide at age thirty-eight.

2007: Transwoman Susan Stanton is fired from her job as city manager of Largo, Florida, after announcing her impending transition.

2008: The first openly transgender mayor of a U.S. city, Stu Rasmussen, is elected in Silverton, Oregon.

2009: Thomas Beatie, a transman from Oregon, gives birth to his second child. Chaz (formerly Chastity) Bono, the only child of Cher and the late Sonny Bono, comes out as a transgender man. Bono is perhaps the first famous person to reveal that he is FTM.

2010: Amanda Simpson is appointed senior technical adviser to the U.S. Commerce Department by President Barack Obama, becoming the first openly transgender person to be appointed to a post in the federal government.

[a] *Lillian Faderman, Horacio Roque Ramirez, Yolanda Retter, Stuart Timmons, and Eric C. Wat, eds., Great Events from History: Gay, Lesbian, Bisexual, Transgender Events, Vol. I, 1848–1983; Vol. II, 1984–2006 (Pasadena, CA: Salem, 2007), 21–22.*

[b] *Susan Stryker, "Dr. Harry Benjamin (1885–1986)," GLBTQ: An Encyclopedia of Gay, Lesbian, Bisexual, Transgender, and Queer Culture, http://www.glbtq.com/social-sciences/benjamin_h.html.*

[c] *Faderman et al., Great Events from History, 108–166.*

[d] *Sanjida O'Connell, producer, Dr. Money and the Boy with No Penis (BBC Horizon, 2004).*

[e] *Minnesota Department of Human Rights, "When Gender and Gender Identity Are Not the Same," The Rights Stuff, Nov. 2006, http://www.humanrights.state.mn.us/education/articles/rs06_4gender_protections.html; Transgender Law and Policy Institute and the National Gay and Lesbian Task Force, "Scope of Explicitly Transgender-Inclusive Anti-discrimination Laws," 2006, http://www.transgenderlaw.org/ndlaws/ngltftlpichart.pdf.*

[f] *Faderman et al., Great Events from History, 320–328.*

Among those involved in the 1969 tumult at the Stonewall Inn was transwoman Sylvia Rivera.[31] Rivera went on to become an activist, helping transpeople of all backgrounds who had been thrown out of their homes. Sylvia's Place, an "emergency night shelter" in New York City for GLBT youth,[32] was named in her honor, as was the Sylvia Rivera Law Project, an organization that advocates for low-income transpeople. Rivera passed away in 2002 at age fifty from cancer.[33]

. . . . .

Lou Sullivan, a transman living in San Francisco, began the first known support group for FTMs and later added a newsletter. Sullivan was also active in the gay rights movement and identified as a gay man. His organization became what is now FTM International.[34] It presently has chapters in eighteen countries, all of which hold support groups for transmen.[35] Sullivan died of complications from AIDS in 1991 at age thirty-nine.[36]

SCIENCE, EVOLUTION, AND GENDER

Although presently there is not a lot of research on the subject, some important scientific discoveries can begin to shed light on transgenderism. Dr. Joan Roughgarden, professor of biology at Stanford University, tackled the subjects of sex and gender and their connection to the natural world in her book *Evolution's Rainbow*. Roughgarden writes: "[P]eople turn to science, trying to use the biological criteria for male to define a man and the biological criteria for female to define a woman. However, the definition of social rests with society, not science, and social can't be made to coincide with biological categories."[37]

Roughgarden goes on to explain that nature proves some important points. She debunks the myth that all natural organisms retain their birth sex for life. The truth is that many plants and animals can be both male and female, biologically speaking, at the same time or at different points throughout their lives. In some species, males actually give birth or females have the exact same chromosomes as the males.[38] Roughgarden writes about some species that have more than two genders and some whose biological structure challenges what we believe is normally male or normally female: "[I]n the spotted hyena, females have a penislike structure externally identical to that of males, and in the fruit bat of Malaysia and Borneo, the males have milk-producing mammary glands."[39]

Clownfish are among those who change sex when the need arises. Female clownfish are normally the ones in charge. When a dominant female passes away, one of the males in the school becomes female and, in the process, becomes capable of breeding. At the same time, a clownfish who was previously unable to breed changes sex to become a male that then is able to breed.[40]

These examples are just the beginning of what nature can tell us about sex and gender diversity in many plants and animals. In a comparison of thirty-four postmortem human brains, scientists found that the part of the brain comprised of a small group of nerve cells thought to pertain to gender and sexuality were similar in transwomen and

Figure 5.1

Source: © *2010 Jennifer Levo. Text of cartoons by Nicholas M. Teich*

non-trans women. Although the study only had one transman's brain, it found that group of nerve cells to be similar to that of a non-trans man.[41]

One can conclude that it might be normal to have variation in sex and gender of people just as it is normal to have variation in sex and gender of animals. Perhaps Dr. Milton Diamond put it best when he said: "Biology loves variation. Biology loves differences. Society hates it."[42]

TRANSGENDERISM AROUND THE WORLD

Transgenderism didn't just pop up in the twentieth century. It has likely been around since the dawn of human expression, long before the written record or biblical times. We are beginning to learn more about how gender may have broken out of the binary throughout history and throughout the world. I will give just a few examples of many that illustrate the existence, and sometimes even reverence, of gender bending. It is important to remember that there are many, many more examples out there.

It has been noted that some Southeast Asian communities in the fifteenth and sixteenth centuries revered males who dressed in women's clothing during certain special ceremonies. At that time the gods that people worshipped were either male or female; it does not seem that there was room for anything else. Nonetheless, these cross-dressing people "served as sacred mediators between males and females and between the spheres of humans and the domains of spirits and nature."[43]

In Thailand, different variations of transwomen include *phuying praphet song* ("second type of woman"), *kathoey* (historically any gender-variant, male-bodied person, but now usually used to describe transwomen), and *ladyboys*[44] (sometimes used as an English synonym for *kathoey*). During the Silla Dynasty in seventh-century Korea, "the Hwarang warrior elite included many boys who dressed as women, wearing long gowns and make-up when they were not practicing archery or preparing for battle."[45]

India's *hijras* have always been known as a third gender. *Hijras* are essentially transwomen (though the identities may not translate 100 percent) who do not, on the whole, have many political rights. They are often not widely respected in India, though times may be changing as they are here in the United States. Many *hijras* point to Shiva, the god of destruction in Hindu mythology, to legitimize their existence and power as a community. Shiva was a strong god known as being "half man and half woman."[46]

In Africa, there is record of belief in gods who transcended gender boundaries in at least twenty-eight different tribes. Male-to-female Zulu spiritual leaders worked alongside women and may still be practicing in parts of South Africa.[47]

In the eighteenth century in Ireland, England, and Wales, transpeople and crossdressers existed in the ruling classes, in agrarian culture, and likely everywhere in between.[48]

TWO-SPIRIT PEOPLE

Many native tribes in cultures indigenous to North America have incorporated transpeople into daily life in different ways. In some cases these people, called *two-spirit* people, were revered because of their gender differentness. Two-spirit people do not usually directly translate to the Western notion of male-to-female or female-to-male (transitioning from one sex to the other). Oftentimes two-spirit people were and are a blend of gender identities, roles, and expressions. Here is one example from Alaska: "The Chugach Eskimo believed that aranu'tiq were two persons united in one, that they were more gifted than ordinary people, and that they were very lucky, like twins."[49]

Two-spirit is a term that was coined in 1990 at gathering of queer aboriginal people in Winnipeg, Manitoba.[50] Some people use it to mean GLBT identities of native or aboriginal people on a broad spectrum, while some use it as encompassing only those on the transgender or gender-nonconforming spectrum. This is in large part because of the fact that Western culture is so different from most aboriginal cultures that it is not always effective, or even possible, to make a direct comparison between the two. The NorthEast Two-Spirit Society, based in New York City, describes two-spirit people in the following way:

In many American Indian communities, men and women['s] styles of speech were distinct; sometimes even different dialects were spoken. The Two Spirit people knew how to speak both in the men and women's ways. They were the only ones allowed to go between the men's and the women's camps. They brokered marriages, divorces, settled arguments, and fostered open lines of communication between the sexes. Their proficiency in mediation often included their work as communicators between the seen (physical) and unseen (spiritual) worlds.[51]

Although this may be true for some aboriginal people, some tribes and nations did not recognize two-spirit people as having these duties or powers.

Prior to the use of the term two spirit, many Western people, mostly anthropologists, used the term *berdache* to describe (usually) male-born, gender-variant people. Berdache is thought of as a derogatory term that originally meant a male sex slave, male prostitute, or a gay man taking on a passive sexual role. Since this is not what two-spirit people are, the term has fallen out of favor.

Let us look at traditional Navajo society as one example of many. In that society, "feminine male" and "masculine female" are two genders distinct from male and female. Feminine males are often associated with typically female gender roles and vice versa for masculine females. A relationship between a feminine male and a masculine male and a relationship between a masculine female and a feminine female are both seen as heterosexual. However, this is not true of contemporary Navajo society, and much of the reason for that is because Western society deems the aforementioned relationships to be homosexual.[52] Traditional Navajo society's view of these relationships shows the blurring of lines between gender and sexuality. Although its structure may allow for more flexibility in gender and sexuality, the juxtaposition of the masculine female with the feminine female and the masculine male with the feminine male comes from heterosexual norms. A relationship between two masculine males or two feminine females, for instance, is not even considered as a possibility in traditional Navajo society.[53]

Many kids in traditional Navajo society did not have to fight the fight that faces our contemporary transgender or gender-nonconforming kids. "Historically, children who showed a keen interest in work tools and activities associated with the gender opposite their sex often were encouraged to develop skills in the occupational domains of their interest."[54] Imagine if our kids were encouraged to be who they wanted to be and do what they wanted to do regardless of gender. Perhaps sometime in the future we will be able to re-create what the Navajos began doing long ago.

Carrie H. House, who is of Navajo and Oneida descent, describes some of the other ways that gender variance was accepted in traditional Navajo society:

> Our oral traditions acknowledge that the he-shes and she-hes (those who hold in balance the male and female, female and male aspects of themselves and the universe) were among the greatest contributors to the well-being and advancement of their communities. They were (and we are) the greatest probers into the ways of the future, and they quickly assimilated the lessons of changing times and people. Recent studies into the lives of contemporary she-hes and he-shes have recovered models or near models of this rich, inventive, reverential, and highly productive approach to keeping balance within a society viewed as an extension of nature.[55]

It is important to note that although House uses the terms "he-she" and "she-he" in a positive light in her description of the Navajo, these are not acceptable terms in contemporary American society; they are thought of as insulting toward transpeople and gender-nonconforming people.

GENDER EXPRESSION IN AMERICA'S EARLY DAYS

Men's and women's clothing did not always look like it does today. In fact, it could not have been more different in some cases.

In colonial times, men wore scarves or neckbands tied in bows, ruffled shirts complete with ruffled sleeves, knee stockings, tight pants, and extravagant long-haired wigs in tight curls tied neatly with a ribbon in the back. Manly? Well, not by today's standards, but at one time, it was.

Women's fashion has changed a fair amount as well. While it was once nearly unheard-of for women to wear pants, it is now the norm. Not too long ago, it was expected that women wear long dresses with corsets underneath. Now, walking down the street in any large city or town, it's likely that only a minority of women are wearing long dresses, and few, if any, with corsets underneath.

Even for babies things used to be different. Pink and blue were "assigned" to girls and boys, respectively, in the twentieth century. But in the nineteenth century most every American baby wore a white dress, which, as Leslie Feinberg writes in *Transgender Warriors*, "didn't seem to skew the gender expressions of these generations of children."[56] What would it be like if the choice of colors were reversed? What if babies in pink, complete with bows, screamed masculinity? We may never know the answer, but one sure bet is that fashion trends will continue to change over the years. Maybe when the United States celebrates its four hundredth anniversary, formal wear for men and women will include tank tops, and who knows what for the rest of America's genders.

As America grew as a country, the North and South developed an extreme ideological split. In 1861, when the Civil War began, all soldiers were male-born and male-identified—or so it seemed. The truth is that women fought in wars throughout the world before they were legally allowed to do so. The Civil War, in both the Union and Confederate Armies, was no exception. Some of these women were discharged for "sexual incompatibility," meaning that someone found out their natal sex by doing a full physical examination (usually upon injury or illness). There were no complete physical examinations prior to enlistment.[57] Perhaps it is true that anatomically these soldiers looked female, but what of their gender identity? This was hardly something that one could bring up in the mid-nineteenth century. Most of these disguised soldiers may have been women who wanted to show their true patriotism; some fought beside their husbands so they would not have to be apart. However, there is at least one famous case (and probably more undocumented ones) of someone who was likely a transman.

Albert D. J. Cashier was born in Ireland and immigrated to the United States. He was labeled female at birth and given the name Jenny

Hodgers, though when he enlisted in the Union army, he did so under the name Albert Cashier. Cashier fought for over three years in approximately forty battles including the infamous siege of Vicksburg.[58] After his service was over, Cashier continued to live as a man. In 1913 a doctor discovered that Cashier had female anatomy, and a barrage of newspaper stories about his "deception" began. In 1914 he was committed to an insane asylum; interestingly, this was because he suffered from dementia, not because he was still living as a man.

"In the end, Albert/Jenny did receive veteran status, but sadly, was shipped to a mental institution and forced to wear female clothing, greatly affecting [his] mental state even more with 'tragic consequences.' At 67 years old, frail and unfamiliar with the finesse of walking in women's clothing, [he] tripped and broke [his] hip. Unfortunately, [he] never recovered from the injury and spent the rest of [his] life confined in bed."[59]

Although this is a sad ending to a life fully lived, Cashier's headstone was engraved with the words "Albert D. Cashier, Co 95 Ill. Inf." and he is honored at Vicksburg National Military Park under this name.[60]

A NOTE ON RESEARCH

Although small-scale studies have been done on trans issues, research continues to be scant. One of the most notable studies to date is the one (mentioned in this chapter) of thirty-four postmortem brains of transpeople outlined in Joan Roughgarden's *Evolution's Rainbow.* Other small studies published in scholarly journals in the last few decades, while helpful, give us only glimpses into the world of transpeople. There are no large-scale, complete long-term studies of lifelong cross-sex hormone use in transpeople in the United States, and there are few if any long-term studies regarding most trans-related issues. This is partly because the topic is so new to the masses, partly because a large number of out transpeople willing to participate in a study may be difficult to find, and partly because the topic is still so controversial. It is difficult to get such research funded for these and other reasons.

A lot of the existing research has been done on the GLBT community. While this is helpful in some respects, the differences between gay, lesbian, bisexual, and trans are so great that it is difficult to lump them together for a study. There is no doubt that trans-related research is picking up and hopefully in the near future we may begin to understand more about the origins of transgenderism as well as health-related and social aspects of trans life.

6

TRANSGENDERISM AS A MENTAL HEALTH ISSUE

The Controversy Over Transgender Identity as a Disorder

Gender identity disorder (GID) appears in the *Diagnostic and Statistical Manual of Mental Disorders* (*DSM*), which is the American Psychiatric Association's official diagnostic book. GID, soon to be changed to *gender dysphoria*, is classified as a mental health condition in which a person desires to be the "opposite" sex of that with which he or she was born. Due to its criteria, many transpeople fall under this diagnosis.

For ease in reading this chapter, try to remember the two acronyms GID (gender identity disorder) and *DSM* (*Diagnostic and Statistical Manual of Mental Disorders*). In the trans community and larger mental health communities, there are those who want to keep GID where it is, those who want to move it out of the sexual and gender identity disorders category and into its own space in the *DSM*, and those who want to remove it completely from the *DSM*. Additionally, some people would rather see it as a medical diagnosis than a mental health one.

The *DSM* is currently in a transitional state from the fourth edition text revision, called the *DSM-IV-TR*, published in 2000, to the *DSM-5*, which is expected to be published in May 2013. *Transsexualism* was first introduced in the *DSM-III*, which was published in 1980. It was replaced by GID in the *DSM-IV* in 1994.

A NOTE ABOUT THE *DSM-IV-TR*

The *DSM-IV-TR* is a 943-page book complete with all official American diagnoses of mental illnesses. Seven of these pages are dedicated to GID. The rest of the volume contains everything from schizophrenia to generalized anxiety disorder to narcissistic personality disorder. GID is in the same section as, and comes directly after, *paraphilias,* which include voyeurism, exhibitionism, and pedophilia, among others.[1] This is expected to change in the *DSM-5*, where GID will become "gender dysphoria" and it will be listed on its own rather than as a sexual disorder.[2] However, even with this change, the condition of gender dysphoria is still classified as a mental disorder by virtue of its existence in the *DSM*.

Homosexuality was in the *DSM* until 1973. It was listed as a "sociopathic personality disturbance" and then got moved to the section on sexual disorders,[3] which is where GID appeared to take its place just seven years after its removal from the book.

GID is included in the *DSM*, used mainly in the United States, as well as in the *International Classification of Diseases* (*ICD*), published by the World Health Organization and used internationally. The ICD includes medical as well as mental health diagnoses. In this chapter we will be dealing only with the *DSM*.

GENDER IDENTITY DISORDER: THE DIAGNOSIS

The diagnostic criteria for GID as written in the *DSM* are the following:

> A. A strong and persistent cross-gender identification (not merely a desire for any perceived cultural advantages of being the other sex).

> In children, the disturbance is manifested by four (or more) of the following:
>
> 1. repeatedly stated desire to be, or insistence that he or she is, the other sex
> 2. in boys, preference for cross-dressing or simulating female attire; in girls, insistence on wearing only stereotypical masculine clothing
> 3. strong and persistent preferences for cross-sex roles in make-believe play or persistent fantasies of being the other sex
> 4. intense desire to participate in the stereotypical games and pastimes of the other sex
> 5. strong preference for playmates of the other sex
>
> In adolescents and adults, the disturbance is manifested by symptoms such as a stated desire to be the other sex, frequent passing as the other sex, desire to live or be treated as the other sex, or the conviction that he or she has the typical feelings and reactions of the other sex.
>
> B. Persistent discomfort with his or her sex or sense of inappropriateness in the gender role of that sex.
>
> In children, the disturbance is manifested by any of the following: in boys, assertion that his penis or testes are disgusting or will disappear or assertion that it would be better not to have a penis, or aversion toward rough-and-tumble play and rejection of male stereotypical toys, games, and activities; in girls, rejection of urinating in a sitting position, assertion that she has or will grow a penis, or assertion that she does not want to grow breasts or menstruate, or marked aversion toward normative feminine clothing.[4]

Let's stop and look at this for a moment. There is clearly a difference between criterion A and criterion B, especially with respect to children. There are kids who may have an "aversion" to stereotypical activities of their birth sex and then there are kids who feel that their anatomy presents a serious problem and also may reject stereotypical activities of their birth sex. This is an important distinction for several reasons. First, many non-trans adult men can say that as kids they rejected rough-and-tumble play, sports, or the like. Likewise, many non-trans women who have never questioned their gender identity were tomboys at some point and then grew out of it. Second, kids who do feel that their genitalia are "disgusting" or severely out of place relative to whom they consider themselves to be are clearly not in the same league as kids who merely reject some of the stereotypical activities common to their birth sex. Put another way, children who experience severe disjunction with their bodies often exhibit signs of depression or anxiety; it is a more serious and immediate matter than simply being a masculine girl or a feminine boy.

There are many trans adults who as children rejected the stereotypical activities of their birth sex but who did not necessarily realize that their genitalia felt alien to them at that time. These people may not have come to grips with their trans identity until later in life. It all goes back to the X-ray example from chapter 3: the relatively few children who fit all of the *DSM* criteria for GID have realized, "Hey, I fell. I'm in pain. I should get an X-ray." On the flip side, the majority of transpeople may know that they are different as kids, but they don't quite know what is going on to make them feel that way, and they may not realize it until much later on in life.

Figure 6.1

Source: © *2010 Jennifer Levo. Text of cartoons by Nicholas M. Teich*

Let's continue with the diagnostic criteria.

> In adolescents and adults, the disturbance is manifested by symptoms such as preoccupation with getting rid of primary and secondary sex characteristics (e.g., request for hormones, surgery, or other procedures to physically alter sexual characteristics to simulate the other sex) or belief that he or she was born the wrong sex.
>
> C. The disturbance is not concurrent with a physical intersex condition.[5]

Another time out for a minute: what does this mean? Though we'll cover the term *intersex* and the related term *disorders of sex development* in more detail in chapter 8, here is a quick definition from the Intersex Society of North America: intersex is a "general term used for a variety of conditions in which a person is born with a reproductive or sexual anatomy that doesn't seem to fit the typical definitions of female or male."[6]

And the last criterion for GID: "D. The disturbance causes clinically significant distress or impairment in social, occupational, or other important areas of functioning."[7]

Exactly what does this mean for a transperson who is very happy with his or her life and does not experience "significant distress or impairment"? Does this person not have GID? Well, here's the kicker: to qualify for gender-affirming surgeries in many countries, one needs to bear some sort of gender-identity-related diagnosis. So transpeople who do not experience distress because of their gender identity may have to pretend that they do in order to get their medical needs covered by insurance. Let's look at the expected changes in the *DSM-5* and how the diagnosis of gender dysphoria compares with that of GID.

GENDER DYSPHORIA: THE NEW DIAGNOSIS[8]

The American Psychiatric Association has proposed some major changes in the GID diagnosis for the fifth edition of the DSM. One of these changes is the name of the diagnosis, which will likely be gender dysphoria. The group of mental health professionals working on the new diagnosis said that the change in name was due to feedback that the term gender identity disorder was stigmatizing.

Gender dysphoria in children constitutes: "A. A marked incongruence between one's experienced/expressed gender and assigned gender, of at least 6 months duration, as manifested by at least 6 of the following indicators (including A1): 1. a strong desire to be of the other gender or an insistence that he or she is the other gender (or some alternative gender different from one's assigned gender)."[9]

Let's stop there for a moment. The addition of a "marked incongruence" in gender "experience/expression" versus "assigned" gender displays a new understanding by the American Psychiatric Association that (a) people have an "experienced gender" that may or may not be the same as that which is assigned at birth, (b) that the term "assigned" is important because it is not the gender someone is "born as" but the one that is assigned to them at birth by (presumably) the adult delivering the baby, and (c) that there are more than just two genders.

Criteria 2 through 7 are similar to what they are in GID, though some wording has changed. Criterion 8 reads: "a strong desire for the primary and/or secondary sex characteristics that match one's experienced gender."[10] The assertion that one's anatomy will spontaneously change, which is in the *DSM-IV-TR*, was removed as a criterion.

Criterion B in gender dysphoria for both children and adults has kept the requirement that one must experience significant distress or impairment, present in GID criteria, but the rest of the wording has changed significantly. Criterion B in gender dysphoria reads "The condition is associated with clinically significant distress or impairment in social, occupational, or other important areas of functioning, or with a significantly increased risk of suffering, such as distress or disability."[11]

In the *DSM-IV-TR*, those who are intersex or have a disorder of sex development are excluded from eligibility for a GID diagnosis. In the new diagnosis of gender dysphoria, the authors have added a subtype to each person who gets the diagnosis: "with a disorder of sex development" or "without a disorder of sex development."[12] Instead of keeping the exclusion in, the authors of the new criteria make it clear that those with disorders of sex development (related to intersex; see chapter 8) can also experience gender dysphoria.

The criteria for gender dysphoria in adolescents or adults has the same "criterion A" as above except that it must be demonstrated by *two* of the following:

1. a marked incongruence between one's experienced/expressed gender and primary and/or secondary sex characteristics
2. a strong desire to be rid of one's primary and/or secondary sex characteristics because of a marked incongruence with one's experienced/expressed gender
3. a strong desire for the primary and/or secondary sex characteristics of the other gender
4. a strong desire to be of the other gender (or some alternative gender different from one's assigned gender)
5. a strong desire to be treated as the other gender (or some alternative gender different from one's assigned gender)
6. a strong conviction that one has the typical feelings and reactions of the other gender (or some alternative gender different from one's assigned gender)[13]

Criterion B remains the same as it is for children, as do the subtypes of with or without a disorder of sex development. Another significant change is a "post-transition" specifier. In addition to the criteria listed above, a person's diagnosis of gender dysphoria can be specified as post-transition if "the individual has transitioned to full-time living in the desired gender and has undergone (or is undergoing) at least one cross-sex medical procedure or treatment regimen. . . ."[14] This specifier does not endorse the aforementioned transition measures as a treatment for gender dysphoria nor does it say that if a person is post-transition that he or she should no longer have the gender dysphoria diagnosis. The post-transition specifier is merely an addendum to the diagnosis for those who have, or are in the process of, living full-time as their true gender.

THE CASE FOR KEEPING A TRANSGENDER-RELATED DIAGNOSIS IN THE *DSM*

Currently in the United States, few insurance companies will pay for transpeople to have gender-affirming surgeries. More often they will cover hormone use, but still, many insurers do not. An increasing number of large corporations are adding health benefits for transpeople, but it is happening little by little.

In places outside the United States where universal health care includes coverage for all surgeries (including gender-affirming surgeries), one has to have a diagnosis to get that coverage. That diagnosis is often GID. This is less relevant in the United States.

Those who believe that transgenderism is a serious mental illness want to keep GID or gender dysphoria in the *DSM*. Many people continue to believe this, despite the growing numbers of healthy, well-adjusted transpeople all over the world. Similarly, many people used to believe that homosexuality was a mental illness. (Obviously some people continue to believe it.) The authors of the *DSM* believe that by definition, transpeople are not mentally healthy, and some would like to see it stay that way.

Another less obvious argument for keeping a transgender-related diagnosis in the *DSM* is that in the United States, mental and behavioral health clinicians can use such a diagnosis to get their patients' therapy sessions covered by insurance. Health insurance companies will often cover psychotherapy if a diagnosis is attached to it. At the same time, many clinicians who do not believe in using GID or gender dysphoria as a mental health diagnosis will instead use other diagnoses such as depression, anxiety, or adjustment disorders to cover the therapy. As was mentioned before, it took until 1973 to rid the *DSM* of a diagnosis of homosexuality as a mental health disorder, so transgenderism may be following that course, just several decades behind.

If a trans-related diagnosis is to remain in the *DSM*, then what is the proposed course of treatment? Well, the *DSM* doesn't specify one, curiously enough, though one might conclude from the specifier at the end of the gender dysphoria diagnosis that gender transition is a normative treatment. However, *Kaplan and Sadock's Synopsis of Psychia-*

try, a bible of sorts for many psychiatrists and a companion to the *DSM*, states the following for adults: "No drug treatment has been shown to be effective in reducing cross-gender desires per se. When patient gender dysphoria is severe and intractable, sex reassignment may be the best solution."[15]

Essentially, this quote endorses giving transpeople the treatment that many of them want and need. Perhaps the reason that "no drug treatment has been shown to be effective in reducing cross-gender desires" is because transgenderism is not an illness at all. Food for thought.

THE CASE FOR REMOVING A TRANSGENDER-RELATED DIAGNOSIS FROM THE *DSM*

So what are the alternatives, if some people need a diagnosis like GID or gender dysphoria to get medical care? One popular option is to make transgenderism a purely medical, rather than psychiatric, diagnosis. The field of endocrinology may be leading the way.

In June 2009, the Endocrine Society, the oldest international organization "devoted to research on hormones and the clinical practice of endocrinology," put out new guidelines for care of trans patients.[16] In a seventy-two-page document, the society explores transsexualism from beginning to end. It recommends that those who have been diagnosed with GID by a mental health professional be treated with hormones and receive a possible referral for sex reassignment surgery if they so desire. In other words, once an endocrinologist has evaluated a transperson who is already said to have GID, he or she then gives a female-to-male transperson a testosterone regimen. In those patients who desire to have surgery, the Endocrine Society further "recommend[s] that the physician responsible for endocrine treatment medically clear transsexual individuals for sex reassignment surgery and collaborate with the surgeon regarding hormone use during and after surgery."[17]

So, what is the significance of this? People still must be diagnosed with GID (or gender dysphoria) to have their endocrinologists follow this protocol. Well, before these guidelines came into being, it was up to each endocrinologist to decide whether a transperson—child or adult—could use cross-sex hormones based on the physician's moral opinion of transgenderism. Now that these guidelines are in place, the practice of endocrinology has a more trans-positive uniformity. However, it is important to note that many endocrinologists do not have training in the area of transgender hormone use and therefore may not feel comfortable taking on a trans patient at all.

Now, another question: what if well-prepared endocrinologists and other medical professionals could evaluate on their own, using professional guidelines, whether a transperson was ready for hormone treatment or surgery without a previous trans-related *DSM* diagnosis? At that point people could simply be evaluated and diagnosed by a medical doctor alone. So why not make GID/gender dysphoria a medical rather than mental health diagnosis? You can be assured that this question is being debated.

Psychotherapists often look to rule out other mental illness in a trans patient. It is important that the patient is truly trans-identified and is not instead suffering from borderline personality disorder, dissociative identity disorder (previously known as multiple personality disorder), or the like.[18] The irony of this is that professionals are ruling out other mental illness so that they can say the transperson has sound enough judgment to make decisions about going through with hormone treatment and surgery. They are ruling out mental illness in order to rule in GID/gender dysphoria. So, again, why is GID/gender dysphoria itself still considered a mental illness?

There are two main points to be argued for making transgenderism a medical diagnosis rather than a mental illness. First, the stigma attached to transgenderism was already great prior to GID's introduction into the *DSM* in the 1980s. Listing it as a clinically diagnosable mental illness furthers that stigma. Changing it to a medical diagnosis would likely reduce the stigma, at least somewhat. Second, which is directly related to the preceding point, is that medical insurers can opt not to cover hormones and surgeries for a mental illness whereas there is a stronger obligation to provide coverage for a medical illness. Currently, insurers often say that gender-affirming surgery or hormone treatment is "cosmetic" and "elective"—and why should insurance companies pay to treat crazy people who want to alter their bodies just because they feel like it?

Because of this, many transpeople cannot afford to physically transition. These people are often forced to live very discontented lives, never being able to become who they truly feel they have always been. Severe depression and suicide are often consequences. A medical diagnosis for transpeople might very well change this and provide help for those seeking surgery and hormone treatment worldwide.

REAL-LIFE SCENARIOS

When I saw young trans or gender-variant clients for therapy, I struggled with the question of whether or not GID was an appropriate diagnosis. I know that it would feel disappointing for many people to see GID stamped on their mental health records. On the other hand, if they did fit the diagnosis, logistically it might help them get what they need.

Let's look at a few examples of young people who went for therapy regarding their gender identity. These are cases that I have come across in talking to others about their work with transpeople. The names and some circumstances have been changed to protect these individuals.

A nineteen-year-old woman who was born male, Danielle, came in for therapy because she was ready to start female hormones and needed a letter to do so. She was getting ready to move to a new state and her endocrinologist required a diagnosis of GID to treat her. The therapist had to think about the most sensible way to go about this. He figured that transparency was the best policy, so he explained to Danielle the pros and cons of giving her an official diagnosis of GID. For Danielle, it ended up being more important to move ahead with receiving hormones than it was to have the potential negative of GID on her permanent record. Obviously, this is not always the case.

A transman in his mid-twenties, Steve, came to therapy for a similar "hormone assessment." He was planning to get on testosterone as soon as he could. However, it was very important for Steve to live stealthily (in such a way that no one would ever know that he was assigned female at birth). He did not want his new employer, coworkers, friends, or acquaintances to know that he was trans. He simply wanted to live as Steve, the person he was always meant to be, without any stigma. This is quite common, but can get tricky. Throughout his childhood and teenage years he was constantly bullied and harassed for being a girl who looked and acted like a boy. This led to several bouts of depression. When he came in for therapy, he simply stated that he could not have GID on his records at all. He and his therapist explored all options for diagnosis and ultimately decided that depression, though it was in remission, was at the time the most appropriate primary diagnosis for him. This way GID did not have to figure into the picture. He then had to find a doctor who would prescribe him hormones without a diagnosis of GID.

A ten-year-old transboy named Derek was being ostracized at school by peers as well as teachers because of his gender identity. The school administration refused to call him Derek or to refer to him as "he" at all. Many people at the school believed that Derek was acting out to get attention. After seeing a child psychiatrist, Derek was diagnosed with GID. The diagnosis was the only thing that then protected him from harassment by students, school officials, and teachers. In this case Derek's diagnosis was used positively, to prove that he was not acting out but that he had a legitimate "condition."

In a show featured on National Public Radio, two approaches to treating gender-variant male-born children were reviewed. One of the children, Bradley, had been treated with *reparative therapy*, a treatment style that seeks to make a transgender or gender-variant child comfortable living as his or her birth sex. The term reparative therapy is not exclusive to gender identity; it is most often used in the context of "curing" homosexuality by seeking to change gay or bisexual people into heterosexuals. The following is part of Bradley's story from National Public Radio's *All Things Considered* show in May 2008:

> [Psychologist Kenneth] Zucker, who has worked with this population for close to thirty years, has a very specific method for treating [trans or gender-variant] children. Whenever Zucker encounters a child younger than ten with gender identity disorder, he tries to make

> the child comfortable with the sex he or she was born with. So, to treat Bradley, Zucker explained to Carol [Bradley's mother] that she and her husband would have to radically change their parenting. Bradley would no longer be allowed to spend time with girls. He would no longer be allowed to play with girlish toys or pretend that he was a female character. Zucker said that all of these activities were dangerous to a kid with gender identity disorder. He explained that unless Carol and her husband helped the child to change his behavior, as Bradley grew older, he likely would be rejected by both peer groups. Boys would find his feminine interests unappealing. Girls would want more boyish boys. Bradley would be an outcast. Carol resolved to do her best. Still, these were huge changes. By the time Bradley started therapy he was almost six years old, and Carol had a house full of Barbie dolls and Polly Pockets. She now had to remove them. To cushion the blow, she didn't take the toys away all at once; she told Bradley that he could choose one or two toys a day. "In the beginning, he didn't really care, because he'd picked stuff he didn't play with," Carol says. "But then it really got down to the last few." As his pile of toys dwindled, Carol realized Bradley was hoarding. She would find female action figures stashed between couch pillows. Rainbow unicorns were hidden in the back of Bradley's closet. Bradley seemed at a loss, she said. They gave him male toys, but he chose not to play at all.[19]

The outcome of this therapy on Bradley's gender identity has yet to be determined, but oftentimes reparative therapy does more harm than good.

THE FUTURE OF TRANSGENDERISM AND THE *DSM*

Just as some transpeople are adamantly against making transgenderism a mental health diagnosis, many do not want to see it as a medical one, either. This is the biggest difference between GID/gender dysphoria and the diagnosis of homosexuality as it was in the *DSM*; gay people were not looking to get hormones or surgery based on their sexual orientation, so, medically, homosexuality was irrelevant.

Some trans advocates are trying to add a clause for GID that if any symptoms such as depression and anxiety are solely due to one's gender identity, and not due to the discrimination and stigma that come from being trans, then GID (or gender dysphoria, as the case may be) should be the diagnosis.[20] If discrimination and stigma do enter into the way a patient is feeling, which they likely would, then anxiety or depression—whatever the patient presents with—should be the diagnosis.[21] The thought is that most people who struggle with their gender identity do so because of depression and anxiety that come from being stigmatized, as I pointed out in the introduction. If this change were implemented, only a fraction of the people now diagnosed with GID would actually retain their diagnosis.

Gender Identity Disorder Reform Advocates, a group of medical and mental health professionals as well as people in many other fields, has suggestions about how to change GID on the whole for the upcoming publication of the *DSM*. This group advocated for the use of the term gender dysphoria. One of the group's ideas is to add a clause for GID "in remission."[22] Remission is "a state or period during which the symptoms of a disease are abated" or diminished.[23] The purpose would be to consider transpeople as in remission if they are being treated with hormones or surgery, since their symptoms of GID/gender dysphoria would likely be gone. If a transperson was diagnosed as being in remission once transition began, then health insurance companies would be obligated to continue covering treatment throughout remission. It would be like any other condition in remission with respect to getting treatment covered by insurance. When someone has cancer in remission, for instance, and must remain on medication to keep the cancer at bay, insurance companies must cover these medications. Adding the specifier "post-transition" is not the same as an "in remission" option.

Another suggestion made by trans rights advocates is to leave open the possibility for a GID/gender dysphoria diagnosis to be removed if and when the time is right. The idea is that if a person is in remission long enough that he or she no longer fits the criteria for GID/gender dysphoria,[24] then the diagnosis may be permanently removed from that person's record.

Even the usually conservative American Medical Association is advocating for transgenderism or transsexualism to be seen as a medical condition. In a resolution passed by its House of Delegates in 2008, it stated: "Gender Identity Disorder (GID) is a serious medical condition. . . . GID, if left untreated, can result in . . . debilitating depression and, for some people without access to appropriate medical care and treatment, suicidality and death."[25] This resolution was a major step in declaring GID a medical, not a mental, issue. The future of GID and gender dysphoria, especially beyond the *DSM-5*, is unclear at this point.

Some countries make up their own minds about what to do. In the spring of 2009, France became the first country in the world to officially remove transsexuality from its list of mental disorders.[26] Who knows; France may have started a trend. Recently, some members of WPATH launched a survey among approximately 200 worldwide organizations that treat and help transpeople, asking whether respondents felt that GID should be removed from the *DSM*. These results were published in 2010: "[T]he majority of respondents felt that the diagnosis should be excluded from the upcoming edition [of the *DSM*]. This negative stand seems to stem from aspects of the diagnosis perceived as harmful to transgender persons."[27] The change in diagnosis from GID to gender dysphoria is simply not the same as complete removal of the diagnosis from the DSM.

The National Association of Social Workers and the American Psychological Association, among many other reputable professional health care organizations, discourage discrimination based on gender identity or expression. In just one example, the American Psychological Association (APA), not to be confused with the American Psychiatric Association (author of the DSM), has the following as part of its laws of governance:

> Therefore be it further resolved that APA calls upon psychologists in their professional roles to provide appropriate, nondiscriminatory treatment to transgender and gender variant individuals and

encourages psychologists to take a leadership role in working against discrimination towards transgender and gender variant individuals. . . APA encourages legal and social recognition of transgender individuals consistent with their gender identity and expression, including access to identity documents consistent with their gender identity and expression which do not involuntarily disclose their status as transgender for transgender people who permanently socially transition to another gender role.[28]

MENTAL HEALTH PROFESSIONALS AND GENDER IDENTITY DISORDER/GENDER DYSPHORIA

Up until very recently, gender identity was a subject not taught in schools of psychology, social work, counseling, or medicine. In most of these places it is still not taught. Therefore, it is largely up to each individual clinician to decide what to think about transgenderism. If clinicians have not been taught exactly what to do in a certain situation, then it is common to turn to their own values and morals. Many clinicians do what they think is right without obtaining information on GID/gender dysphoria. This can be dangerous. What if a medical doctor decided that although she had never seen anyone with her patient's condition, she would do what she deemed to be "right," so she proceeded without gathering factual information on the subject? I would venture to say that would fall under the category "unethical," or at the very least it would be pushing the limits of a doctor's Hippocratic Oath. Mental health professionals have the same duties to do right by their patients. But just as transgenderism is still new to the public, it is still new to many clinicians who began practicing long before there were classes or seminars on transgenderism.

Kelley Winters presents a poignant example of this in her book *Gender Madness in American Psychiatry*. In an example from 1995, an adult male-to-female woman was interrogated by psychiatrists who were treating her as a man.

> One psychiatrist demanded, "Are you a homosexual? Do you wish to become one?" When [the transwoman] responded "no," that she was attracted to women, the doctor was incredulous. Reflecting old stereotypes confusing sexual orientation with gender identity, he responded, "Well, then, why are you doing this [becoming a woman]?"[29]

Without proper knowledge of gender identity, some clinicians end up doing great harm to their patients. They are, after all, in a position of power.

To this point, I recently received a call from a mental health counselor in the southeastern United States who had her first-ever transgender client: a twelve-year-old. She said that she looked at a popular book about psychotherapy with children and saw that its suggestion about transkids was a reparative approach; in other words, it said that trying to force the child to become happy with the sex he or she was assigned at birth was the correct method to use. On her own, she came to the conclusion that there had to be a better way and she began looking for trans-positive resources. Just as easily, she could have taken the advice of the book and, in turn, her client's life might have been negatively affected.

CLINICIANS AS GATEKEEPERS

When following the WPATH Standards of Care, one of the jobs of a health care professional seeing a trans client is to write a letter supporting the client's decision to go on hormones or have surgery. We learned about this in chapter 4, but we didn't discuss what it means to have to ask permission. The new version of the Standards of Care eliminated a requirement for psychotherapy, per se, but an assessment by a professional is still necessary. Let's say you have a transman who has known he was a man for the past thirty years but couldn't start to transition until now because of his life circumstances. Instead of going straight to a doctor to obtain hormones or make a surgical appointment, he must first consult with a therapist or physician and "convince"—for lack of a better word—the professional that he understands the risks and benefits of the transition procedures.

Some call these clinicians *gatekeepers* because of their power to control who gets treatment. Many transpeople ask questions like this: What if someone needed back surgery so he could walk properly again? He would expect to have it right away. Now imagine that person having to obtain documentation in order to make sure that he knew the "consequences" of being able to walk and was of sound enough mind to make the decision to have the surgery. This process can feel degrading and frustrating.

But, by the same token, some people may need time in therapy or with a physician to talk things over before going ahead with medical procedures. In therapy, success depends a lot on the relationship between client and therapist. All health care providers need to be knowledgeable about how gender issues affect people's lives and transpeople must be patient in order for both parties to feel satisfied. Clinicians, of course, are under no obligation to write a letter recommending hormones or surgery. The provider may request more time or deny the request based on his or her best professional opinion. Hence, the cynically used title "gatekeeper."

A NOTE ABOUT SEXUAL ORIENTATION

The *DSM* says that "virtually all" females with GID—usually transmen—will be attracted to females.[30] This is a vast generalization and an incorrect one, at that. Many transmen are attracted to all types of men. No specific percentage is available, but it is much higher than the *DSM* makes it out to be.

Why does the *DSM* care about whom someone is attracted to? Actually, the *DSM-IV-TR* calls for all adults diagnosed with GID to have a specifier of either "sexually attracted to males, sexually attracted to females, sexually attracted to both, or sexually attracted to neither."[31] Seemingly realizing the irrelevance of sexual orientation in transgenderism, the American Psychiatric Association's Sexual and Gender Identity Disorders Work Group suggested that the *DSM-5* remove this specifier altogether.

7

DISCRIMINATION

Exploring the Barriers That Transpeople Face

Picture yourself having a conversation with someone whose gender you did not know. Would you be able to pay attention to what that person was saying, or would you be spending all your energy asking yourself, "Is that a man or a woman?" Why is it so important to answer that question? As human beings and, more specifically, as people living in a modern Western society, we place an enormous amount of stock in knowing whether someone is male or female. But if you step back and think about it, it is seldom, if ever, necessary to know a mere stranger's sex or gender identity. Still, we feel the need to constantly categorize. Whether or not you are keenly aware of it, constant thoughts swirl in your mind when you interact with people. "I am speaking to a woman in customer service right now." "I am ordering a cup of coffee from a man right now." "I am having a conversation with the new employee at work—a transgender person—right now. The person is now a woman but she used to be a man. I wonder what she was like as a man. I wonder if her family and friends accepted or rejected her. I wonder if she has had surgery." When speaking to a transperson, your thought trail may distract you from the purpose of the interaction in the first place. Maybe your new trans coworker complimented your shoes or she asked you if you knew anyone with an extra ticket to the ballgame tonight. But, through no fault of your own, you are now thinking about which bathroom this person will use at work and, by the way, how *does* this person go to the bathroom? If you start to feel uncomfortable at this point, you would not be alone. But if you think about what is occurring, it may be your own thought pattern that is making you uncomfortable. Is it that this person is supposed to be something that he or she isn't? If so, where does this notion of "supposed to be" come from?

There is a reason that children often take the news of a person's gender transition more easily than adults do. In fact, the younger the child, the more easily it can roll off his or her back. Why is this? We are taught from a very young age that boys belong here, doing these things, in this way, and that girls belong there, doing those things, in that way. As we grow with that ingrained in our mind, we take it for granted that there is no other way to be. Our thinking about gender in these black-and-white terms becomes commonplace; so much so that few of us ever really think about it. The younger we are, the fewer years we have lived in this black-and-white space, and the more room there is for new ideas. For a six-year-old, it may make sense that "Aunt Sally always felt she was a boy, so *he* will now live as one." For a forty-year-old, that prospect becomes harder to envision. "Aunt Sally was born a girl and is therefore a woman. That's how it goes." These patterns of thinking are not true of everyone, of course.

Let's go back to your coworker who asked if you had an extra ticket to the ballgame tonight. While you may be thinking about what is under her dress or what hormones are surging through her body, she is patiently waiting to hear if she'll score a seat at tonight's Red Sox–Yankees game. Human beings are all similar in many ways. However, because of negative stereotypes assigned to transpeople, some people do not even think of them as human beings. Anything that challenges social norms can make us feel uncomfortable. Gender is thought to be one of the most basic components of a person, if not *the* most basic. You might think, if you can't even get a grasp on someone's gender, how can you get a grasp on any part of that person's life? This thought pattern, and the ultimate questioning of what gender means, gives many people such a fright that they can do nothing but place transpeople in an "other," or even a "freak," category. When someone causes us to stop and think about what our own gender means for us, it can be a downright scary prospect. Once we see a group of people as "other," it becomes all too easy—even excusable to some—to discriminate against that group.

When we think about transpeople within other marginalized groups, such as incarcerated transpeople or transpeople seeking shelter from domestic violence, not many of us will think about the negative impact that being trans has in these situations. But, unfortunately, the reality is that it is difficult for any transperson to maintain dignity and self-respect in these cases. Where do we separate "men" and "women"? What happens if a transwoman who is *pre-op* or *non-op* (has not had surgery) gets put in a men's prison? You can be sure that violence is a major probability. What about a transman who needs to seek respite in a shelter for those affected by domestic violence? Most of those shelters are for women only. If any are available for men, and again the person is pre-op or non-op, then he may be rejected from all sides. It is true that many women may feel threatened by the presence of a man in such a shelter. But how can this transman's needs be met? These conversations are ongoing within social justice organizations. There is no getting around the fact that the gender binary of men and women—as we always knew it—is not the reality. Therefore, steps must be taken to ensure the safety, well-being, and a chance for the all-important "pursuit of happiness" for transgender and nontranspeople alike. Nondiscrimination laws help move us in this direction.

NONDISCRIMINATION AND HATE CRIME LAWS

Specific laws pertaining to nondiscrimination for transpeople vary widely from state to state, county to county, city to city, and town to town. Sixteen states and the District of Columbia all have a gender identity antidiscrimination law on the books.[1] The states are California,

Colorado, Connecticut, Hawaii, Illinois, Iowa, Maine, Massachusetts, Minnesota, Nevada, New Jersey, New Mexico, Oregon, Rhode Island, Vermont, and Washington.

We like to take solace in the fact that law enforcement and emergency services are on our side, and many of us take it for granted that they will be there if a problem arises. This is not necessarily so for the transgender population (and many other marginalized populations). One story about a young woman named Tyra Hunter makes us think about this point no matter how we feel about transpeople. Hunter was living in the Washington, DC, area. In 1993 she was in a car accident and emergency personnel responded to the scene. When they took her clothes off to help her, they realized that Hunter was anatomically male. Witnesses in the trial said that the emergency responders walked away and were joking about the situation. Hunter later died of her injuries.[2]

The 1999 Hollywood blockbuster *Boys Don't Cry* was the true story of the life and eventual murder of Brandon Teena, a young transgender man who was labeled female at birth and began living as a man in rural Nebraska. He was living stealthily; no one knew that he was anatomically female. Teena did not take hormones, nor did he have any trans-related surgeries at the time of his death. He was raped and killed by two former friends who found out that he was anatomically female. Unfortunately, these stories are not rare enough. Teena and Hunter's stories are merely two examples; they barely scratch the surface of the horrific crimes committed against transpeople.

In October 2009, President Barack Obama signed into law the Matthew Shepard and James Byrd, Jr. Hate Crimes Prevention Act. The namesakes of the bill were both victims of hate crimes who died; the former for being gay, the latter for being African American. This bill expanded the existing federal coverage of hate crimes to include sexual orientation, gender identity, sex, and disability.[3]

Often mentioned alongside this hate crimes bill is the *Employment Nondiscrimination Act* (*ENDA*). ENDA "prohibits employment discrimination on the basis of actual or perceived sexual orientation or gender identity by covered entities (employers, employment agencies, labor organizations, or joint labor-management committees)."[4] This inclusive version of ENDA has yet to be passed in Congress. Until it is, people in many places throughout the country can lose their jobs or their ability to get a job because they are GLBT.

What about transgenderism as a disability? Some argue that transgenderism can be considered a physical or mental disability. However, calling transgenderism a disability is controversial on several fronts. First, many transpeople reject the notion that they are disabled in any way. Second, some people with disabilities reject the idea that transgenderism can be considered a disability. Third, the jury is still out as to whether there is conclusive evidence that transgenderism is a biological condition. Many disabilities have been shown to be caused by a specific set of events, whether those events occur in utero or later in life. Evidence about the cause of transgenderism is simply not available yet, and it may never be. Despite this controversy, transpeople can try to make a disability claim when experiencing discrimination,[5] but the Americans with Disabilities Act specifically excludes any protection for people with gender identity disorder. According to Shannon Minter, an attorney who works on many transgender-related cases for the National Center for Lesbian Rights, there are transgender kids who have gained access to the appropriate bathroom in their schools using the Individuals with Disabilities Education Act because this accommodation would not be provided using any other means.[6]

THE BATHROOM DEBACLE

Imagine resigning yourself to not ever using the bathroom in a public place. For transpeople, this is often a reality. Those who are in transition or do not *pass* on the outside as "clearly male" or "clearly female" are thrown out of both men's and women's restrooms on a daily basis. Some places provide "unisex" or "family" restrooms, but the majority do not. If a transperson wants to go out and enjoy a concert, sporting event, or simply a day outside the home, he or she must make concessions that most people never have to think about. As one transperson put it, whose experience is not unique: "I learned how not to use a bathroom from the time I left in the morning to the time I got home, and sometimes that was more than ten hours."[7]

Personally speaking, I have yet to use a public restroom where people have walked around naked. There are private stalls (at least there are supposed to be) in every bathroom, and at urinals, well, the code of conduct is to always keep your eyes at eye level or on yourself. At a recent fund-raiser for the camp that I run for transgender youth, U.S. Congressman Barney Frank made an amusing observation. To paraphrase, he said he recently challenged his colleagues in Congress to find him one person who grew up in a household with non-unisex bathrooms.

Transgender people and bathroom use has become a national debate. Several states are now contending with transgender-inclusive nondiscrimination bills in their legislatures. The opposition often dubs these acts "Bathroom Bills" and argues that they will enable men to dress as women, come into women's restrooms, and prey upon our wives and daughters.

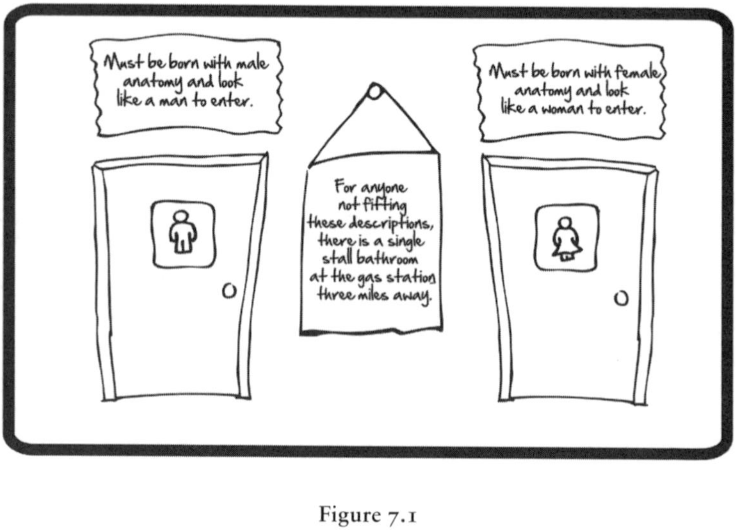

Figure 7.1

Source: © 2010 Jennifer Levo. Text of cartoons by Nicholas M. Teich

First, these bills are meant to accommodate transpeople in public places, which include restrooms. The purpose of these accommodations is so that no person is forced to hold it in for hours on end or have to hunt for a single-stall restroom in a gas station or similar place. These laws are not meant to, nor will they, accommodate predatory behavior.

Second, places that have made the leap to ban discrimination in public accommodations, including restrooms, report no uptick in the number of men dressing as women and trying to assault people. Lisa Mottet, director of the Transgender Civil Rights Project at the National Gay and Lesbian Task Force, inquired about such occurrences to several states that have implemented such nondiscrimination laws. The Washington state Human Rights Commission responded that it is "not aware of any circumstances in which people have inappropriately tried to access locker rooms, restrooms or other gender-separated facilities because of the gender expression/identity protections under the [Washington law]."[8] The Iowa Civil Rights Commission similarly responded that it has "simply not been informed of any such occurrence."[9] And the list goes on.

Finally, it has always been illegal to assault anyone in a restroom or elsewhere, no matter how someone is dressed and no matter what bathroom he or she uses. The law against assault has not changed and will not change because of a trans-inclusive antidiscrimination law.

CUSTODY ISSUES

Transgender parents who separate from or divorce their partners face an uphill battle with respect to child custody. In some cases the two parties are able to work out custody amiably, but especially for those whose separation is due to a partner coming out as transgender, it can easily turn into an ugly situation. The stereotypes of transgender people can get the better of a judge, especially if he or she has not dealt with the subject before. For instance, let's take a transwoman who biologically fathered one or more kids with her (at the time, his) wife. Let us say that the marriage is dissolved after this father comes out as a woman and the wife does not want her former husband to have any contact with the kids from that point forward. In many courts in America, it would be easy for the wife to argue that her former husband is a pervert and not fit to have any contact with their children. Since most people are not well acquainted with trans individuals, the likelihood that someone would believe this stereotype is fairly high. After this transwoman has lost her partner and presumably some family and friends during her transition, she has now lost her children as well.

In the book *Transgender Rights*, attorney and law professor Taylor Flynn outlines a case about a couple made up of a non-trans woman and a transgender man. The man had transitioned before they got married and subsequently adopted his wife's one-year-old child that she'd had previously. Then they had one child together through artificial insemination. Upon their separation after ten years of marriage, the non-trans partner argued that her husband was "really a woman" and that he should have no legal rights to the children. This was in Florida, where same-sex marriage is illegal and same-sex partner adoption was illegal at the time. In the end, the court of appeals ruled that his marriage and adoption of the first child were void and he was found to have no rights to the child that they had together, either.[10]

Transgender adults and children face many similar issues, but a large number of their difficulties are different due to the stage of life they are in. While trans adults struggle with employment, trans kids struggle in school.

NEGATIVITY THAT TRANSGENDER KIDS FACE IN SCHOOL

It has become clear to us as a country that bullying in schools is out of control. Children are bullied for a number of reasons, and one of the most common relates to gender identity. You may know that phrases such as "you are so gay," "sissy," "fag," "dyke," "man up!" and so on are pervasive in American youth culture. Although they may seem to be directed toward sexual orientation, as we learned in chapter 2, it is really gender that cues someone to think another person is too girly, sissy, or a faggot (in the case of a boy).

A 2009 study by the Gay, Lesbian and Straight Education Network (GLSEN) showed that harassment based on gender is pervasive. This sad reality does not come as a surprise to anyone, but it is worth noting some of the details of this study, which is the first of its kind. GLSEN found that 90 percent of transgender students reported hearing fellow students comment about someone not being masculine enough or feminine enough on a regular basis. Furthermore, more than a third of trans students heard school staff make negative remarks about gender identity. Only 11 percent reported staff intervening when kids made negative comments about gender identity. A whopping 82 percent of trans students felt unsafe at school. When surveyed, it was found that 46 percent of trans students had missed at least one day of school within the past month because they felt unsafe at school.[11] How can a student survive, much less thrive, in an environment filled with such hostility?

Although there has been no separate study on religious schools, we can guess that discrimination against trans kids might be worse because of some of the belief systems that are in place. Let's take a brief look at religion and trans discrimination.

RELIGION AND TRANSGENDER DISCRIMINATION

Although we like to believe that a clear separation of church and state was written into the Constitution, it was not. Many courts throughout the years have interpreted the First Amendment's clause on freedom of religion to mean that there is a distinct separation of religion and governing laws, but the original phrase of a "wall of separation" between church and state was merely written in a letter from Thomas Jefferson to a group of Baptists in New England. It was never part of a law. Therefore, the battle rages on. Religion continues to shape many contemporary belief systems and laws. What do religions say about transgenderism? In America, where Christianity is the dominant religion, what does the

Bible say? It probably depends on who is interpreting it. The passage that I have most often heard used against transgender people comes from the Old Testament. It says: "A woman shall not wear anything that pertains to a man, nor shall a man put on a woman's garment; for whoever does these things is an abomination to the Lord your God" (Deuteronomy 22:5). This is more an issue of *gender expression* rather than *gender identity*. Some literalists take this to mean that women should never even wear pants. If we take a look at some other Bible passages, we see that meanings have changed with the times. The following are not allowed according to the Bible, and some of these "offenses" are even punishable by death: getting divorced, marrying a woman who is not a virgin, wearing clothes made of two different materials such as wool and linen, cursing your mother or father, shaving your beard and sideburns, and eating shellfish. Yet some people, ignoring all of the above and more, still point out the few passages pertaining to what they see as modern-day transgenderism or homosexuality.

Religion has, at times, been used to incite fear, whether purposely or not. Most of those who object to nondiscrimination laws for transpeople use the Bible and other scriptures as their reasoning. Fundamentalists make up a relatively small group of people in the United States, yet their voices are louder than any others when it comes to rejecting nondiscrimination laws. Some Christians, Jews, Muslims, and members of other religions feel as if the fundamentalists in their respective religions are taking over and drowning out the voices of the masses. There are many accepting religious and spiritual folks who are pro-nondiscrimination for transpeople and other marginalized populations. In Christianity, one such denomination is the United Church of Christ.

In 2003 the United Church of Christ adopted a resolution on including transgender people in the church. This resolution begins: "Whereas, God has brought forth human beings as creatures who are male, female, and sometimes dramatically or subtly a complex mix of male and female in their bodies" and ends with this:

> Therefore be it resolved that all congregations of the United Church of Christ are encouraged to welcome transgender people into membership, ministry, and full participation; and [b]e it further resolved that

> all settings of the United Church of Christ are encouraged to learn about the realities of transgender experience and expression, including the gifts and callings and needs of transgender people, and are encouraged to engage in appropriate dialogue with transgender people.[12]

Although such a resolution is rare, we may see them begin to pop up more and more in progressive denominations of different religions.

In 2003, American V. Gene Robinson was the first openly gay bishop consecrated by any branch of the Anglican church (he is an Episcopalian) anywhere in the world. Reverend Dr. Cameron Partridge, a transman and Episcopal priest, reflects on his experience within the Episcopal church in the context of Robinson's consecration:

> The [Episcopal church's] sense of theological depth and richness . . . [and] emphasis on recognizing and honoring the dignity of all human beings was a huge help to me as I came to terms with my trans identity.
>
> I came out as trans, quite inconveniently, while I was in the ordination process as well as a first year doctoral student. I had begun the ordination process as [an] openly gay [woman], but then came out to my bishop as trans about a year before the hoopla surrounding Gene Robinson's consecration began. As I watched events and debate unfold—debates that never included any naming of trans concerns or issues even though conceptions of gender norms were always in the mix, often under the rubric of sexuality—I wondered what was in store.
>
> I was ordained a deacon in June 2004 and a priest in January 2005. With the support and aid of a group called TransEpiscopal, Integrity USA, and other Episcopal groups committed to social justice, we have been able to bring greater awareness of trans concerns and communities to the wider Episcopal and Anglican table. The challenge has been huge; getting people to even say the word "transgender" or "trans" has sometimes been an uphill battle. But, that is starting to change. In 2008 I joined four other trans people at the Lambeth (bishops) Conference's "Fringe Festival" on a first of its kind panel entitled "Listening to Trans People," which was part of the wider Anglican "Listening Process" regarding issues of gender and sexuality. Then, at

> the Episcopal Church's General Convention in 2009, I joined a group of lay and ordained transgender Episcopalians from across the U.S., where we worked toward the passage of several supportive resolutions. The Episcopal Church is now on record in support of an inclusive Employment Non-Discrimination Act, and for passage of local and state trans nondiscrimination laws. We still have much work to do to move forward, particularly regarding ordained ministry. While there are several openly trans priests and deacons, our ministry canons need to be amended to explicitly support that reality and leaders and communities around the country need basic education about our lives. But when I consider how completely unnamed and unknown trans people were in the Episcopal Church when I was beginning transition, I am truly amazed at how far we have come in five short years.[13]

The future of the Anglican Church is anyone's guess, but it is clear that splits within many churches and denominations will continue to occur as long as one faction wants something radically different than another.

Religions have views on transgenderism that are often vastly different from one another and ever changing. Differentness is at the core of the argument over accepting or not accepting transpeople in many religions. But transpeople are hardly the first group to be seen as different.

IMMIGRATION, RACE, AND TRANSGENDERISM

In 1790 the United States took its first census. People in each household were counted in the following categories:

1. Free White males of 16 years and upward
2. Free White males under 16 years
3. Free White females
4. All other free persons
5. Slaves[14]

Now fast forward eighty years. Slavery is officially over, but political correctness has not exactly arrived. The following races and ethnicities were counted in the 1870 census: "White, Black, Mulatto, Chinese, Indian." The form asked the value of the person's real estate, it asked about literacy, and it asked whether the person was "deaf and dumb, blind, insane, or idiotic."[15] Twenty years after that, the census form was changed to ask if the person was "crippled, maimed, or deformed" (and if so, what were the details) and whether the person was a "prisoner" or "pauper."[16]

In 2010 the U.S. Census Bureau decided that the definition of marriage on the form included anyone who was partnered or in a long-term relationship and wanted to count themselves as "married." The bureau even made T-shirts marketed to gay and lesbian Americans, helping them declare to the country that they were going to count their "wife" (for women) or "husband" (for men) even though same-sex marriage is not federally recognized by law. The bureau spent a good amount of resources in helping GLBT folks to feel comfortable filling out the census as themselves. But, in reality, nothing except the marriage question had changed. There were no questions about sexual orientation or gender identity, and the age-old two-checkbox "male" and "female" part remained. I was approached at a queer event by someone working for the Census Bureau who was trying to get the word out that it was important for all GLBT people to fill out the form. I asked what the difference was for transgender people between this form and all past census forms. The Census Bureau representative said that transgender people can be counted for the gender with which they identify. I repeated my question because this was no different than any forms dating back to the first one that counted both men and women. Though she had no real answer, she assured me that the bureau wanted to make sure that all GLBT people were counted. The National Gay and Lesbian Task Force started a campaign called "Queer the Census" and provided stickers for the outside of the census envelope to declare to those counting that the resident was lesbian, gay, bisexual, transgender, or a "straight ally." The stickers may have been a good idea for inclusivity and visibility, but they are not officially counted as part of the census.

Will 2020 bring more gender options to the form? It may be too soon to ask for transpeople to be counted, and we may never get an accurate count anyway. Many people who might by definition be considered transgender actually consider themselves to be strictly male or female—however they identify—and would not check a "transgender" box even if it was available. But if we can move from "free" versus "slave" to "maimed" and "idiotic" to "married even if to the same sex," who's to say what future census forms will look like?

As we know from census forms and many other sources, race has always been an important part of a person's identity in America. Even now, in this country, with the election of the first African American president behind us, we still struggle with racism in nearly every area of life. Imagine that you are transgender and black. You have been raised as a girl and a woman, but you feel like a man. If you take the leap to physically transition, you will then take on—through no choice of your own—all the stereotypes that face black men in America. People may cross the street when they see you walking near them. Women may clutch their purses tightly when they notice you. Though many innocent black men struggle with these issues on a daily basis, they may be new to you as you begin to be seen as a man. As if you did not have enough to take on with a gender transition, you must now contend with being scrutinized and possibly blamed needlessly because of what you represent. Now imagine—or perhaps you don't have to imagine—that you are of any race or ethnicity that values its men a lot more than its women. You were labeled male at birth but are now transitioning to female, because that is who you really are. Obviously this adds complicated and uncomfortable layers to the already difficult gender transition process.

People immigrating to America must face their own set of difficult circumstances. But what if you were a trans immigrant? A person who is being persecuted or who fears persecution can seek asylum in the United States based on "membership in a particular social group."[17] According to the National Center for Transgender Equality, many transpeople have gained asylum in the United States because of their gender identity. In many countries people face the real possibility of execution because they are transgender. Once in the United States, besides the discrimination a transgender immigrant may face in housing, employment, and other areas, he or she must make sure that all documentation bears the correct name and gender. Those trans immigrants who expect Americans to greet them with warmth, acceptance, and guaranteed safety as a polar opposite to what they may have experienced in their home country will have to deal with a sharp learning curve.

TRANSPEOPLE IN THE U.S. MILITARY

According to the Transgender American Veterans Association and the Servicemembers Legal Defense Network, someone will likely be deemed medically unfit for service if it is discovered that he or she is trans during a routine military physical exam. (Unlike what we learned about the Civil War in chapter 5, routine medical exams today are extensive and thorough.) If someone has not had surgery but it is discovered that he or she is transgender, that person would likely be deemed mentally unfit to serve. The Servicemembers Legal Defense Network, which seeks to put an end to GLBT discrimination in the military, goes on to say:

> Transgender individuals who are already in the military and who are thinking about beginning their transition should think twice about this decision. The military currently has a strong bias against service by transgender individuals and is unlikely to provide the medical support necessary for transitioning service members. The medical and mental health regulations described above apply to currently serving individuals, so even if transgender service members seek treatment from civilian health care providers, they are at risk because they have a duty to report such treatment to the military. Failure to abide by these regulations could result in criminal prosecution by the military. Also, the military strictly regulates uniform and grooming standards by gender. "Cross-dressing" or perceived "cross-dressing," even in the context of following medical protocol in advance of full transition, will probably be considered a violation of military regulations and result in discipline, discharge or criminal prosecution.[18]

This is a stern warning to active-duty trans military members that not only should they be concerned about being "out" on the job, they should expect negative consequences.

Additionally, because sexual orientation and gender identity are often (though wrongly) thought to be one and the same, some transgender people have been discharged under "Don't Ask, Don't Tell," which was originally written to exclude gay, lesbian, and bisexual service members.

Retired U.S. Navy Lt. LeAnna Bradley has eighteen medals and eleven ribbons and citations from her thirty-seven-year service. She also happens to be transgender. After joining in 1955 as a seventeen-year-old boy, she spent over two years in Vietnam as a Seabee (the construction battalion of the navy). There she was wounded twice and spent over four months recovering in a body cast.[19] During her time in the navy, LeAnna was not known as "LeAnna" nor as a "she." It wasn't until she was sixty years old that she finally made the transition from male to female. LeAnna reflects with cautionary optimism: "One can only hope that transgender people will one day be able to serve this great country with the pride and honor that was instilled in me in the beginning of my service career."[20] In 2009 LeAnna was honored at an American Veterans for Equal Rights event in Chicago. She plainly said: "In combat it makes no difference who or what you are. . . . We are there to do our job for our country and our families."[21] Time will tell if the U.S. military will someday agree with LeAnna.

"PASSING" AND ITS RELATIONSHIP TO DISCRIMINATION

There is a saying in the transgender community: "FTMs pass in the streets; MTFs pass in the sheets." What exactly does this mean? Well, it's important to note that here we're only talking about FTMs who have been on testosterone for some months and have had top surgery (or who can hide any semblance of breasts that they might have) and MTFs who have been on estrogen for a while and have had lower surgery as well.

Average people on the street who walk by an FTM will not think that they have just passed by a transgender person. Testosterone and lack of breasts makes a person look male—and to someone who doesn't think about the diversity of gender on a daily basis, this means an assumption that the person was born male. This is clearly not always the case. However, once a transman who has not had lower surgery takes off his clothes "in the sheets," it is clear that he was not originally assigned the male sex.

MTFs often, but not always, have a harder time passing in the streets. If puberty has already hit by the time a natal male transitions to female, she may be much taller than most other women and may have developed traditionally male features that female hormones cannot change. These include but are not limited to large hands, full facial hair (electrolysis is often necessary), and more prominent or angular facial features. However, "in the sheets," an MTF who has had lower surgery is often indistinguishable from a natal female.

Though transpeople have a good chance of facing discrimination in their lifetime, it will likely not be this way forever. The greater the number of people who understand that transpeople are more like them than they are different, the better the chances that they will treat transpeople equally.

8

LESSER-KNOWN TYPES OF TRANSGENDERISM

Understanding Cross-Dressers, Genderqueer People, Drag Queens, and More

---

Have you ever noticed that nearly every form we fill out asks us to choose one, male or female? Everything else is presented as an open-ended question, or at least has more than two options. With such a diverse planet, and each human being unique, why must we force ourselves into two cramped boxes when it comes to sex and gender?[1] My wish is that forms would ask us to write in our gender just as we write in our name. There are too many of us with too many identities to be suffocated by just two options.

Transsexualism, or transitioning from one sex to another, often with hormones and surgery, is only one type of transgenderism. Although it is often used synonymously with the term *transgender*, as we know, there are many more people than just transsexuals who fall under the umbrella of transgenderism.

GENDERQUEER

We are going to start out with *genderqueer* because the term is growing in popularity to describe, for the most part, people who feel that they are in between male and female or are neither male nor female. Well, you might ask, what does that mean exactly? In the simplest terms, it means that, for example, a person who was labeled female at birth feels that he or she is not a woman but not exactly a man, either. This can be confusing for many, including the genderqueer person, especially in the beginning. However, this does not mean that this person is perpetually confused about gender identity. He or she may feel genderqueer permanently; in other words, it is not always a stepping stone to full transition. People can be perfectly clear that their gender is genderqueer, and that is how they live their lives. At the same time, the label of genderqueer is a common stopover for those who are not sure whether they are going to transition and are trying to figure out their true gender identity.

Is it difficult to be genderqueer out in the world? Absolutely. We've talked about pronouns, bathrooms, and other day-to-day issues earlier in this book. If you are genderqueer, those issues are constant, especially if you present as someone who is in between a typical man and a typical woman.

People often find the notion of genderqueerism difficult to understand. They may hear that a genderqueer person is in between male and female, or is neither, but they may continue to ask, "Okay, so what sex or gender does that make them, really?" This is where it is perhaps most difficult to live as a genderqueer person. The constant explanations that sometimes get nowhere can be frustrating and disheartening for genderqueer people. For instance, what pronoun does a genderqueer person use? Well, it depends on personal preference. Some will use "he" or "she" because they are easiest to use in public or because one fits better than the other. However, some genderqueer people use altogether different pronouns such as "ze" (instead of he or she) or a singular "they" (as in "they went to the store today" when referring to only one person). Some will make up their own pronoun that may be unique to them.

Some will prefer to use only names and no pronouns, which can become awkward: "Jamie went to the store today. Jamie bought some grapes and oranges, then Jamie brought them out to Jamie's car." Well, you get the point. Using any alternative pronouns besides he or she requires a lot of time and effort in terms of explaining them. Sometimes people do not want to make gender the focus of their task, so if someone in a store refers to the genderqueer person as "he" or "she" and the person does not want to engage in a discussion of gender and pronouns, the person may let it slide. At the same time, it can be demoralizing, just as it is to "mispronoun" any person.

There are also many people who identify as genderqueer transmen or genderqueer transwomen. They may identify as men or women, but with a component of genderqueerness; they don't fit into the binary of "just man" or "just woman." Micah Domingo, a self-labeled genderqueer transman, describes himself:

> From my vantage point, I can see the binary in a clear way. With this perspective, I have the honor of blending the binary and creating something completely new and different. To others, I am a mystery of gender, an in-betweener, a gender nomad. The fact that I love musicals is not a gendered act. Neither is playing video games, making sure I look pretty, reading *Vanity Fair*, being on stage rapping, tying my shoes, wearing a suit and tie, or dancing. I do have a masculine leaning, but I tend to stray away from anything that reinforces the gender binary. I know that none of those activities, or any activity, is only for one gender. I am capable of doing anything I want and still identifying as male.[2]

An important note: there are many people who fit the definition of a genderqueer person but do not call themselves genderqueer, either because they do not like the word or because they don't feel it fits them. They may refer to themselves as gender variant, gender nonconforming, androgynous, a myriad of other terms, or they may use no terms at all. It is important to let people define themselves rather than be labeled by someone else.

GENDER VARIANT OR GENDER NONCONFORMING

The terms *gender variant* and *gender nonconforming* are similar, and the use of one or the other really comes down to personal preference. Any transgender person can be considered gender variant or gender nonconforming because he or she, by definition, does not conform to Western society's notion of what a male or a female is. A person assigned male at birth who is very feminine and may like to dress in feminine clothes or participate in typically female activities, but who still identifies with his birth sex, might be gender variant or gender nonconforming. The term is usually used for people assigned male at birth because it is more obvious when a man engages in stereotypically feminine behavior than it is when a woman engages in stereotypically masculine behavior. This is because of our society's lenience toward tomboyishness, especially in childhood, and rejection of most boys or men who enjoy feminine or female things. Gender variant or gender nonconforming can, however, be used to describe a female person who expresses herself as masculine yet still identifies as a woman.

Many gender-variant or gender-nonconforming people do not self-identify as such. These terms are often directed at natal male children who like "girly" or feminine behaviors, interests, or clothing. Although gender-variant and gender-nonconforming people fit under the umbrella term of transgenderism, we know that the term transgender is often used interchangeably with transsexual; therefore many of these gender-variant people are not labeled as transgender, per se.

Gender-nonconforming people are distinct from transpeople (transsexuals, that is) in that they may not feel as though their genitalia or secondary sex characteristics are foreign or as if they do not belong to their bodies. It is unknown why some people are gender variant or gender nonconforming but not transsexual,[3] just as it is unknown what causes any aspect of transgenderism.

As we discussed in chapter 2, gender variance, especially with respect to *gender expression*, usually connects us with terms like gay or lesbian. Many gay, lesbian, and bisexual people are what you might consider gender variant. No matter what one's sexual orientation is, life can be extremely difficult for those who live in the middle ground on gender. As the author of an article on transgender youth writes: "While there is space for such identities in some cultures, mainstream American culture is not one of them."[4]

CROSS-DRESSERS

Cross-dressers are often confused with transsexuals as well as with drag queens or drag kings. There are several things that differentiate these terms. In short, cross-dressers are people who dress in clothing typically reserved for the "opposite" sex, either in the privacy of their own home, in places with other cross-dressers, or out in public. Cross-dressing is still widely known as transvestism, which is now considered a pejorative term. A person who cross-dresses should not be known as a *transvestite*, but as a cross-dresser.

When we think of cross-dressers, what images do we conjure up? A man in a dress? A man in women's underwear or pantyhose? How about a woman in a jacket and tie? The latter image is probably far less commonly thought of, but that person can also be called a cross-dresser.

Statistics on cross-dressers are hard to come by. Most people do it privately and thus are not inclined to take a survey or tell people about it. Many cross-dressers have partners or spouses who are not aware of their cross-dressing, at least in the beginning. Sometimes a partner or spouse will find an article of clothing that does not belong to him or her but seemingly does not belong to the spouse either, and this can bring up a myriad of issues. Often the first thought is that the cross-dressing partner is actually having an affair. For instance, if a cross-dressing man is married and his wife finds a pair of women's panties that don't belong to her, she may jump to the conclusion that he is having an affair. Many spouses end up eventually finding out about the cross-dressing whether on purpose or by accident, and it can put a strain on the marriage or partnership. Some spouses will wonder whether the cross-dresser will eventually transition to the opposite sex, or whether this is a phase, or even whether it is a mental illness.

There is a diagnosis in the *DSM-IV-TR* called *transvestic fetishism*, also knows as *autogynephilia*. It is essentially when a man cross-dresses for sexual pleasure. However, many people cross-dress because it makes them feel more genuine, and they do not get sexual pleasure from it, nor do they intend to transition to the opposite sex. There is a great deal of shame involved in cross-dressing. It is ingrained in us as small children that cross-dressing is wrong. Even a young boy who consistently puts on his mother's pantyhose and makeup knows that he should never tell her about it.[5]

Due to the shame associated with cross-dressing, many people sometimes purge their wardrobe of all the clothes and accoutrements associated with their cross-dressing. In other words, a man who cross-dresses may take all female-associated items out of his wardrobe and throw them away, hoping that this will stop his urge to dress in women's clothes. It is possible that cross-dressing can be a phase, but for many people, it is something that they do long term. Therefore, many of those who purge their wardrobes end up replacing what they have thrown out, starting the cycle over again. Other reasons for purging might include fear of someone finding out about the cross-dressing, fear that a gender transition is inevitable, or fear that the person's relationships will be damaged if it continues.

Many relationships do survive cross-dressing. Helen Boyd, author of *My Husband Betty* and wife of a male cross-dresser, writes about her thoughts on the subject:

> Crossdressing is not necessary to a person's survival, but it does seem to be necessary to his well being. Crossdressing is not, as some wives of crossdressers might wish, a selfish whim. Crossdressers as a group do not give it up despite the troubles it can cause in their lives. The phenomenon is stubbornly inexplicable, a cross between a compulsion and a wish.[6]

Each relationship handles cross-dressing differently. The following is part of the story of another woman who is married to a male cross-dresser:

> I found out about my partner's gender issues a little over five years ago right after our fourteenth wedding anniversary. We come from healthy, well-functioning, wonderful, church-going, middle/upper-middle class families. . . . I had virtually no clues about his "feminine side." . . . I resented the times Joe had been away on business with his [feminine] clothes. It was like he had a fantasy woman I couldn't compete with.[7]

This woman questioned whether it was worth it to stay in her marriage, but she ultimately decided to. She placed restrictions on her husband's dressing that he agreed to because it meant that his wife would stay with him. Many spouses of cross-dressers never come to fully understand their partner's inclinations nor do they accept the cross-dressing unconditionally. As with any issues that arise in relationships, each couple decides the best course of action to take. Another wife of a male cross-dresser, whose husband came out as such on their first date, said the following: "When we go out together, if there is something that he is wearing or doing that is obviously feminine I will point it out if it makes me uncomfortable. On the other hand, I will try and make him prettier when he wants to dress around the house."[8]

Virginia Erhardt, author of *Head over Heels: Wives Who Stay with Cross-Dressers and Transsexuals*, the source of the previous two stories, believes that women who know about their male partners' cross-dressing from the beginning have a better shot at staying in the relationship.[9]

Just as there are cross-dressers who do or do not derive sexual pleasure from the act of dressing in clothes associated with the opposite sex, there are also cross-dressers who are not shamed by the idea of dressing. They do not feel dysphoria about their bodies or their identities, and they see cross-dressing as a part of their lives just like any other hobby that is intertwined with their identity. Some cross-dressers take on a different name when they dress. Many will adjust their mannerisms, including voice, to fit the gender expression that they take on. For men who cross-dress, wigs, shaving legs and underarms, breast stuffing, jewelry, and makeup (among other accessories) are part of the experience.

So, what is the relationship between cross-dressers and transpeople (namely, transsexual people)? Well, although it may seem that cross-dressing is a step toward gender transition, the two groups remain dis-

Figure 8.1

tinctly different. It certainly can be a step toward transition, but in many cases cross-dressing exists on its own. In fact, there is a divide between many transwomen and male cross-dressers specifically; some transwomen believe that cross-dressers are too afraid to transition while some cross-dressers think that transwomen are merely cross-dressers who have gone too far. This tension is not unlike the divide between some butch lesbians and some FTMs. But regardless of these hostilities, the fact remains that transwomen who live full time as women are not the same as men who cross-dress occasionally. Transwomen are women, plain and simple. Explains one male cross-dresser: "I have no illusions about who I really am. I know that I am a guy, but sometimes it just feels nice being a girl for a while. It has been a part of me all my life, and I suspect it always will be."[10]

DISORDERS OF SEX DEVELOPMENT AND INTERSEX

People with *disorders of sex development* (*DSD*), sometimes called *intersex*, include those who used to be referred to as *hermaphrodites*.

The term hermaphrodite, derived from the Greek mythological child Hermaphroditus, is now considered pejorative and should no longer be used. Hermaphroditus was the offspring of Hermes and Aphrodite and was "portrayed in Greco-Roman art as a female figure with male genitals."[11] "True hermaphroditism" was, until recently, a term used to describe a condition in which a person has both testicular and ovarian tissue.[12]

According to the Intersex Society of North America (now the Accord Alliance), intersex "is a general term used for a variety of conditions in which a person is born with a reproductive or sexual anatomy that doesn't seem to fit the typical definitions of female or male."[13] But even the Intersex Society of North America officially moved to using the term disorders of sex development to encompass all intersex conditions. Just as in other areas of transgenderism, certain people have a preference for some terms over others. If someone prefers the term intersex over DSD then it is important to respect that.

For the purpose of simplicity in this chapter, I mostly use the term DSD. According to Children's Hospital Boston, people with DSD have "medical conditions where average sexual development does not occur. DSD can include . . . medical issues that may make it difficult to determine a child's sex or conditions that interfere with a patient's sexual and reproductive function."[14] Another definition of DSD is that such disorders are "congenital conditions in which development of chromosomal, gonadal, or anatomic sex is atypical."[15] Though one might think it is rare that a child is born with such a condition, it is estimated that 1 in every 1,500 births is a baby with DSD.[16] In fact, in the animal kingdom, excluding insects, one-third of all animal species are what we might consider intersex.[17] Again, this shows how varied animals are. Human bodies vary too, which makes perfect sense, but social stigma prevents these variations from being normalized in our society.

Causes of DSD are not always known, but may include mutations of chromosomes or genes, or over- or underexposure to certain hormones while the fetus is developing in the uterus.[18] Treatment of DSD depends on the specific condition and is always changing with new research. For infants born with ambiguous genitalia, the protocol used to be to do immediate surgery to make the child's anatomy look typically male or female, depending on several factors. Nowadays doctors often try to persuade parents to hold off on surgery and to assign the child a gender identity based on an experienced medical team's best conjecture. Parents should keep an open dialogue with their child as he or she grows older, and if the wrong gender was assigned or the child wants genital surgery, a decision can be made at that point. When a child with ambiguous genitalia is born, it is rarely a medical emergency. Unnecessary surgery on infants can result in a lifelong loss of genital sensation as well as fertility problems. Obviously, this can severely negatively affect a person's life.

Many DSD advocacy groups currently recommend deferring surgery until a person can make his or her own informed decision (especially in the case of ambiguous genitalia) and letting the person with DSD and his or her parents have complete access to medical records.[19] It may seem silly to even mention the latter recommendation, but many people with DSD have grown up with the facts shielded from them, whether by medical professionals or their own caregivers. It is the duty of parents or caregivers to be forthright with a child who has DSD.

It is important to know that although historically intersex/DSD has fallen under the transgender umbrella, many people believe that it should not be included. There can be transpeople (transsexual or otherwise) who are born with DSD and the two identities remain distinct. Some people are not aware that they have DSD, nor are their parents or doctors. It could be a chromosomal abnormality that has no outward effects. In this case, those who transition away from the sex they were assigned at birth might first and foremost identify as trans and then later may come to find out that they actually have DSD. This does not necessarily change their trans status. People choose their own language according to what feels right. As we know, some transpeople with or without DSD consider themselves just men or women and do not feel the need to acknowledge the fact that they passed through some atypical steps to become who they truly feel they are. On the flip side, many people with DSD do not consider themselves trans and may not wish to be associated with the GLBT community. They may view their DSD as a medical disorder only.

Many of those who are born with DSD are labeled, at birth, with the sex that corresponds to their gender identity. In other words, they are non-trans like the majority of the population, and may be able to lead a very typical life. For many, DSD is a private medical issue that need not be discussed at all. Others find solace in support groups. It may depend on the severity of the DSD. For example, someone with ambiguous genitalia who was forced into surgery as an infant likely has different emotional needs and concerns than someone whose DSD never affected his or her appearance and was successfully treated with hormone replacement therapy. Likewise, a person born with DSD may have been labeled as one sex but always felt like another, so he or she might undergo a gender transition much like a transperson without DSD. That person may consider themselves trans as well as having DSD/being intersex.

You might wonder how a person who is not 100 percent male or female in the typical sense could transition from male to female or vice versa. The fact is that virtually all babies born with DSD, no matter how severe, are given a gender identity via the physicians' and parents' best guess, so that he or she may grow up "normally." These kids can be boys or girls just like everyone else. Some of these people may grow up and realize that they have a gender identity that doesn't match up with the sex they were assigned at birth. Since they have lived as one sex and everyone knows them as such, they may undergo a gender transition like any other transperson.

Raven Kaldera, a self-described trans/intersexual FTM, was labeled female at birth but identified as a boy and ultimately transitioned to become one, though he was actually born intersex. Kaldera described part of his experience in a book that has the subtitle *Voices from Beyond the Sexual Binary*:

> I feel like that much of the time, one foot in each world, frantically juggling opposite elements. Not just male and female either; there are also the separate countries of hormones and culture, intersex and transgender, spirituality and intellectualism, queer and transsexual, and so forth. The lines aren't stable; they move around, but they're easy to find. Just come and look for me. Where I stand, there's the line. Where I move, the line goes with me. I live on it. It is imprinted into my flesh. You can take my clothes off and see for yourself.[20]

DRAG QUEENS AND KINGS

Drag queens and *kings* are always associated with performance. If you ever get confused between cross-dressers and people who do drag, remember that drag is for a performance. Legend has it that *drag* was originally an acronym for "DRessed As a Girl," which was used in theater stage directions when women were not allowed to be actors (so men always played female roles). Of course, this was solely in reference to drag queens, before the advent of drag kings.

Drag queens are men who dress as women and perform as women. Though drag has historically been most popular in gay circles, one need not be gay to do drag. Similarly, drag kings are women who dress as men and perform. Most drag queens sing, lip-synch, dance, or do skits of some kind. Many drag queens impersonate female pop stars and vice versa for drag kings. People who do drag on a regular basis often have a drag name (a name for the woman or man that they become) and sometimes a drag personality.

There are drag troupes that travel around or do shows on a regular basis at a nightclub or other establishment and have large followings. All the Kings Men, a group of traveling drag kings based in Boston, bills itself as an "all female, character-based performance troupe that creates wholly electrifying cabaret-style and modern vaudevillian productions . . . [made up of drag kings] who collectively play between thirty and fifty gender bending characters per performance."[21] There are annual national and regional pageants for both drag queens and drag kings.

Daniel Harris, author of *Diary of a Drag Queen*, begins his story with the following: "I have never wanted to be a woman, and I do not want to be one even now that I am trying to be one. . . . I have never had any doubts about my manhood, never been plagued by gender confusion, never felt like a 'woman trapped in a man's body.'"[22] Harris illustrates the clear distinction between being a drag queen as a performer and being a transsexual woman. This is not to say that there are not some drag performers who have a different take on their own gender. Some might use it as a stepping stone to transition, but some know that they just like to do it for show and will never live full time as the gender in which they do drag. Others might feel like they fall somewhere in between those two.

As a young boy, Chris Hagberg used to dress as a woman for Halloween. As he got older and came out as a gay man, he dabbled a bit in drag both on the stage and off. When he became involved in a gay men's softball league, he acquired the drag nickname "Momma Kitty," partially due to his maternal nature. To Chris, Momma Kitty and he are different in some ways but the same in many ways. He often dresses in full drag and becomes Momma Kitty for softball league events, including fund-raisers. There is one thing that Chris always notices: "Momma Kitty is her own entity, but it's really interesting to see how people interact with me when I'm not in drag as opposed to when I'm in drag. People approach me differently when I'm Momma Kitty—there's absolutely no two ways about that."[23] Chris mainly does drag for fun, but he contends that it is an interesting experiment in gender's impact on approachability. Apparently, everyone is more talkative with Momma Kitty than they are with Chris. They will stop Momma Kitty on the street or at an event and start a conversation with her; they will confide in her with an almost automatic trust. When Chris changes back into his regular clothes and walks by the same people, they usually don't recognize him. When he asks, "What, do I have to wear a dress to get you to talk to me?" they realize that it's the same person they see before them, but they are still not willing to open up like they did when he was dressed as Momma Kitty. Chris believes that the Momma Kitty persona has helped him understand gender in a way that he never did before. His advice: "I think everyone should do drag once."[24]

Now that you have learned a bit about other types of transgenderism that fall under the trans umbrella, hopefully you are armed with more knowledge than you had coming in. But before you go, I have a few final thoughts.

PARTING WORDS

In America, we have seen that teenage suicide because of bullying has reached epidemic proportions. Many of these kids are GLBT, and most of them are taunted due to some component of their gender expression.

I hope that you will talk to others about what you have learned about transgenderism. No one should have to suffer because of who he or she is, but we know that reality tells us differently. People have been bullied and persecuted for who they are since the dawn of time. But we are not defenseless. The more education that is out there about what it means to be different, the better.

Maybe the next time you run across a form that asks if you are male or female, you will think about the absurdity of this question. If we consider the continua of gender identity and gender expression, there is really an infinite number of ways to be. Not everyone puts themselves in categories that have been described in this book. People can fall into all categories, some categories, one category, or no categories at all. What is important is realizing that human beings are incredibly complex creatures and gender is just one part of what makes us each unique.

APPENDIX A

Glossary

Affirmed female: Someone who identifies as female but was not labeled female at birth.

Affirmed male: Someone who identifies as male but was not labeled male at birth.

Anatomical sex: The physical structure of one's body that usually makes a person male or female. It is often used to refer to the sex that someone was labeled at birth, since people are usually labeled male or female due to the appearance of their genitalia.

Androgynous: An androgynous person has a *gender expression* and/or *identity* that blends the stereotypically male and female traits.

Asexual: An asexual person does not have romantic attractions toward people of any sex or gender.

Autogynephilia: See *transvestic fetishism*.

Berdache: A pejorative term that was once used to describe gender-variant people, often in North American aboriginal cultures. It is a French word that has origins in terms like "sex slave" and "submissive boy."

Bigender: People who identify as both men and women, neither, or somewhere in between the classical two sexes.

Bisexual: A bisexual person is attracted to men and women.

Bottom surgery/lower surgery: Includes any number of genital surgeries that a transperson might undergo.

Breast augmentation (mammoplasty): Surgery in which breasts are constructed or breast tissue is added, usually by implants.

Chest surgery: This can refer to mammoplasty, but usually refers to female-to-male procedures (see *top surgery*).

Chondrolaryngoplasty: See *trachea shave*.

Cisgender: People who are cisgender are not transgender; their gender identity matches up with the sex they were assigned at birth. The vast majority of people are cisgender.

Coming out: The short form of "coming out of the closet," which originally referred to the act of revealing one's sexual orientation. It is now more widely used to refer to revealing anything that someone has been hiding. Many transpeople use it to talk about revealing their trans identity.

Cross-dressers: People who enjoy wearing clothes typically associated with the opposite sex. Some people dress in private, some in public. This term usually refers to men who dress as women but can refer to women who dress as men, as well.

Diagnostic and Statistical Manual of Mental Disorders (DSM): The American Psychiatric Association's handbook on all diagnosable mental disorders.

Disorders of sex development (DSD): Any of several conditions that make the body develop atypically with relation to the person's sex. A DSD may or may not manifest itself externally (e.g., ambiguous genitalia). In some cases people do not know that they have a DSD until they seek medical care, sometimes for an unrelated condition. DSD is closely related to the term *intersex*.

"Don't ask, don't tell": A policy first implemented in 1993 stating that *gay*, *lesbian*, and *bisexual* troops were unable to serve openly in the U.S. military. The name of the policy refers to the rule that no one could ask servicemembers if they were gay or bisexual and no gay or bisexual servicemembers should tell anyone if they had a sexual orientation other than *heterosexual*. This policy was repealed in September 2011.

Double-incision mastectomy with male chest reconstruction: A type of *top surgery* for *transmen* in which breast tissue is removed via two incisions below the breasts. Then a male-looking chest is constructed (nipples are resized and placed in a typically male position). There are also natal males who have this surgery for a medical condition in which they have more breast tissue than the average male, called gynecomastia.

Drag kings: Women who dress up as and impersonate men, usually for entertainment. The term *drag* is thought to have originated as an acronym for

"DRessed As a Girl," specifically because *drag queens* existed before drag kings.

Drag queens: Men who dress up as and impersonate women, usually for entertainment.

Dyke: A word that has historically been used to refer to lesbians derogatorily, but which is often used now within the lesbian community in a positive manner.

Employment Nondiscrimination Act (ENDA): An act introduced in the U.S. Congress, which has not yet passed, that includes sexual orientation and gender identity in federal employment nondiscrimination policies.

Facial feminization surgery: Any number of surgeries that a male-to-female transperson might undergo to make her face have a more naturally feminine appearance. These procedures can include reshaping the nose, chin, brow, cheeks, and any other part of the face.

Faggot: A word that has historically been used to refer to gay men derogatorily.

Female-to-male: Transgender people who are assigned female at birth and transition to live as men.

FTM (F2M): The shortened form of *female-to-male*.

Gatekeeper: In the context of transgenderism, this term refers specifically to doctors and therapists who hold the power to prescribe hormones and/or surgery in the transition process.

Gay: The preferred word to refer to *homosexual* men and often homosexual women as well.

Gaydar: An invented word referring to a person's sense of whether another person is gay. Typically gay people are said to have gaydar, though some nongay people profess to have it as well.

Gender: The "behavioral, cultural, or psychological traits typically associated with one sex."[1] However, gender may include the behavioral, cultural, or psychological traits associated with the sex one is assigned at birth (for someone who is not transgender), the opposite sex (for someone who is transgender), or anywhere in between.

Gender-affirming surgery: Any one of many surgeries that may affirm a transperson's gender identity. This can include genital, facial reconstruction, chest, or other surgeries. Gender-affirming surgery may be referred to as *sex change*, though this is an outdated and largely incorrect term.

Gender binary: The notion that there are only two sexes and genders: male and female.

Gender dysphoria: The feeling that one's gender does not match the sex that was assigned at birth, leaving the person unhappy with the assigned sex (and usually his or her body). *Transsexual* people often suffer from gender dysphoria unless or until they transition. The term gender dysphoria is expected to replace gender identity disorder in the fifth version of the *Diagnostic and Statistical Manual of Mental Disorders*. Its criteria are listed in chapter 6.

Gender expression: The external representation of one's gender identity, usually expressed through feminine or masculine behaviors and signals such as clothing, hair, movement, voice, or body characteristics.[2]

Gender identity: One's internal sense of who one is; being a woman or man, girl or boy, or between or beyond these genders.[3]

Gender identity disorder (GID): A diagnosis in the *Diagnostic and Statistical Manual of Mental Disorders-IV-TR* that is given to many transpeople. Its criteria are listed in chapter 6. See also *gender dysphoria*.

Genderqueer: A term that describes people who feel that they are in between male and female and/or are neither male nor female, or reject the *gender binary* altogether. It is a term that should be used only if a person self-identifies as such.

Gender reassignment surgery (GRS): See *gender-affirming surgery*.

Gender role: A set of duties and/or lifestyle that is common to one gender or sex. Historically, a typical gender role for a man would be to work and be the breadwinner, while a woman's role would be to take care of the home and children. Gender roles are constantly changing in American society.

Genital reassignment surgery (GRS): Specifically, the genital part of *gender-affirming surgery*. This may include *metoidioplasty*, *phalloplasty*, *vaginoplasty*, or a number of other procedures.

GLBT (or *LGBT*): Gay, lesbian, bisexual, or transgender (the order may be switched). There may be additional letters such as Q (*queer* or questioning), I (*intersex*), and A (allies).

Harry Benjamin International Gender Dysphoria Association: The earlier name of the *World Professional Association for Transgender Health (WPATH)*. It was named for Dr. Harry Benjamin, who was known as the "father of transsexualism."

Hermaphrodite: A pejorative term no longer in use that referred to someone who had both typically male and female tissue. See *intersex* and *disorders of sex development (DSD)*.

Heteronormative: A society in which heterosexuality is the norm; in some cases it is considered the only acceptable sexuality. The United States is considered a heteronormative society.

Heterosexual: A person who is primarily attracted to people of the opposite sex (see *straight*).

Hijra: A transwoman in India (although the term transwoman may not exactly match hijra). Hijras do not, on the whole, have many political rights. They often stick together in living and working situations.

Homosexual: A person who is primarily attracted to people of the same sex (see *gay*).

Hysterectomy: The removal of the uterus, sometimes along with the ovaries, fallopian tubes, and cervix (often called a complete hysterectomy). This is a common surgery for FTMs.

International Classification of Diseases (ICD): A diagnostic manual for physical and mental health conditions, maintained by the World Health Organization, that includes statistics and information on worldwide health issues.

International Journal of Transgenderism: Scholarly, peer-reviewed journal of the *World Professional Association for Transgender Health (WPATH)*.

Intersex: A person born with some atypical biological characteristics that are both male and female. This can manifest itself in ambiguous genitalia, development of secondary sex characteristics that are inconsistent with genitalia, atypical chromosomes (XXY or XYY, for example), or in many other ways that are different from the classic development of a male or female. Intersex people used to be called *hermaphrodites*, which now considered a pejorative term. The term *disorders of sex development* is now favored by intersex people in many circles.

Kathoey: A term usually used in Thailand to describe transwomen, though historically it has described any natal male whose *gender expression* was feminine. In English, this term is sometimes translated as *ladyboy*.

Kinsey Scale: A scale of sexual orientation developed by Dr. Alfred Kinsey. It ranges from 0 to 6, 0 being completely heterosexual and 6 being completely homosexual. Kinsey argued that many people fall between 0 and 6, not only on 0 or 6.

Ladyboy: See *kathoey*.

Lesbian: A woman who is attracted to other women. Some women prefer the adjective *gay* to the noun lesbian, and vice versa.

Male-to-female: A transgender person who was assigned male at birth and transitioned to live as a woman.

Mammoplasty: See *breast augmentation surgery*.

Metoidioplasty: A *bottom surgery* procedure for an *FTM* whereby the clitoris, which has been enlarged by testosterone, is released so that it extends out farther, resembling a small penis. The urethra can be extended and rerouted through the new penis so that urinating in a standing position is possible.[4]

Metrosexual: A term that describes *straight* men whose *gender expression* is more feminine than that of the stereotypical straight man.

MTF (M2F): The shortened form of *male-to-female*.

Natal sex: The sex that someone was labeled with at birth, usually based on appearance of external genitalia.

Non-op: A term for transgender people who do not have any surgery as part of their transition.

Oophorectomy: The removal of the ovaries, often performed as part of a hysterectomy for an *FTM*.

Orchiectomy: The removal of the testicles, a procedure for an *MTF* that is done in conjunction with or independent of a *vaginoplasty*.

Pansexual: A person who is attracted to people of any and all genders.

Paraphilia: "A pattern of recurring sexually arousing mental imagery or behavior that involves unusual and especially socially unacceptable sexual practices."[5]

Pass: A transperson who can pass is perceived to be the gender that he or she feels that he or she is. For example, a female-to-male transperson who passes is perceived by the public as being just like any other man.

*Periareolar (*or *keyhole) surgery*: A type of *top surgery* for an *FTM* in which an incision is made around the nipple and breast tissue is removed.

Phalloplasty: An *FTM bottom surgery* procedure in which a penis is constructed using skin from another site on the body (abdomen or forearm, for example). If the skin donor site is the forearm, a penis is created with a "tube-in-tube technique" while the skin is still attached to the arm.[6] It is then moved to the pubic area. Often a phalloplasty is accompanied by the closing of the vagina, extension of the urethra through the new penis so that the person may urinate while standing, and creation of a scrotum with testicular implants inside.[7] The completion of a phalloplasty usually includes multiple surgeries.

Phuying praphet song: A Thai term that roughly translates to mean a transwoman. It literally means "second kind of woman."[8]

Pre-op: A term for transgender people who have not yet had surgery as part of their transition but who plan to in the future.

Queer: A catchall word for those who are *gay, lesbian, bisexual, transgender,* questioning their sexuality, or who do not fit into the *heterosexual* or male-female binary world. Many people are still sensitive about the word, and it is most often used by younger generations because it has such a negative history.

Reparative therapy: A type of psychotherapy designed to keep a transperson in the sex and gender that was assigned at birth. This is highly controversial and often damaging to the person. The term is also applied to a type of psychotherapy designed to make a *gay* or *bisexual* person *heterosexual*.

Sex: "Either of the two major forms of individuals that occur in many species and that are distinguished respectively as female or male especially on the basis of their reproductive organs and structures."[9] But sex can also mean *intersex,* or someone with a *disorder of sex development* who is not categorized as specifically male or female. Sex is not fully explained by its dictionary definition. According to some people, organs and structures do not dictate sex just as they do not dictate gender. For example, if someone asked a female-to-male transgender person what sex he was, he would likely respond male, regardless of the fact that he might still have typically female organs. So, if someone feels that he is a man (gender), he would likely also consider himself male (sex).

Sex change: A commonly used but usually incorrect term for *gender-affirming surgery.*

Sex reassignment surgery (SRS): See *gender-affirming surgery.*

Standards of Care for the Health of Transsexual, Transgender, and Gender Nonconforming People is a document maintained by the *World Professional Association for Transgender Health (WPATH).* These standards, sometimes known as the Harry Benjamin Standards of Care, were written mainly for medical and mental health professionals. They are currently in their seventh version since the first printing in 1979.[10] The Standards of Care are not binding by law but they are the closest thing to a universal standard that exists for trans health care. See appendix B to learn how to obtain a full copy of the Standards of Care.

Stealth: A term for a transperson who lives as the gender that he or she transitioned to and does not reveal his or her transgender status.

Stonewall: On June 28, 1969, police raided the Stonewall Inn, a "gay bar" in Manhattan's Greenwich Village neighborhood. These types of raids on *GLBT* bars were commonplace, but this time the patrons of Stonewall fought back, and chaos ensued. *Stonewall* became the name of a movement that jumpstarted organized GLBT rights in America.

Straight: See *heterosexual.*

T: A term for testosterone used in the *FTM* community. It may also refer to the term *transgender* in *GLBT.*

Top surgery: Surgery that an *FTM* may undergo to have a male-looking chest. See *double-incision mastectomy* and *periareolar.*

Trachea shave: A procedure in which an *MTF* has her Adam's apple reduced to look more feminine. This is a component of *facial feminization surgery.*

Tranny: A usually derogatory term for a transgender person. Although some transpeople use this word positively, many do not find it acceptable.

Trans: Literally, "across"; a short form of *transgender* or *transsexual.*

Transgender: Today, an umbrella term for many different identities. People who are transgender have a *gender identity, sex,* and/or *gender expression* that does not line up with the sex they were labeled with at birth.

Transgenderism: The noun form of *transgender* (adjective).

Transition: In this book, the process that some transgender people undergo to live as the *gender* and/or *sex* that they feel they are, rather than the sex they were assigned at birth.

Transman: See *female-to-male.*

Transsexual: A person who identifies as the opposite *sex* of that which he or she was assigned at birth. Most transsexual people, but not all, take hormones and/or have surgery to change their appearance.

Transvestic fetishism: A condition listed as a disorder in the *Diagnostic and Statistical Manual of Mental Disorders-IV-TR* in which a man dresses in women's clothing, usually for the sake of sexual arousal. This diagnosis will likely be changed in the fifth version of the manual.

Transvestite: A term that should no longer be used. The correct term is *cross-dresser.*

Transwoman: See *male-to-female.*

Two spirit: Some people use this term for *GLBT* identities of North American native or aboriginal people on a broad spectrum, while some use it to refer only to those on the *transgender* or gender-nonconforming spectrum. This is in large part because contemporary Western culture is so different from most aboriginal cultures that it is not always effective, or even possible, to make a direct comparison between the two.

Vaginoplasty: An *MTF bottom surgery* procedure in which a vagina is created out of penile skin. In most cases the penile skin is essentially turned inside out to form the lining of the new vagina.[11]

World Professional Association for Transgender Health (WPATH): The governing body of the WPATH *Standards of Care*. It was originally named the Harry Benjamin International Gender Dysphoria Association. WPATH is made up of medical doctors, psychologists, social workers, counselors, and other helping professionals who work with transpeople. It also publishes the *International Journal of Transgenderism* on a quarterly basis.

APPENDIX B

Resources for Readers

Watchdog/Legal Organizations

Gay and Lesbian Advocates and Defenders (GLAD),
(617) 426-1350,
www.glad.org

Gay and Lesbian Alliance Against Defamation (GLAAD),
(323) 933-2240 and (212) 629-3322,
www.glaad.org

Human Rights Campaign, Transgender Issues,
(800) 777-4723,
www.hrc.org/issues/transgender.asp

National Center for Lesbian Rights,
(415) 392-6257,
www.nclrights.org

National Center for Transgender Equality,
(202) 903-0112,
www.transequality.org

National Gay and Lesbian Task Force,
(202) 393-5177,
www.ngltf.org

Servicemembers Legal Defense Network,
(202) 328-3244,
www.sldn.org

Transgender Law and Policy Institute,
www.transgenderlaw.org

Transgender Legal Defense and Education Fund,
(646) 862-9396,
www.transgenderlegal.org

Health-Related Organizations

American Medical Association, GLBT Advisory Committee,
www.ama-assn.org/ama/pub/about-ama/our-people/member-groups-sections/glbt-advisory-committee.shtml

American Psychological Association, LGBT Concerns,
www.apa.org/pi/lgbt/index.aspx

Association for Lesbian, Gay, Bisexual and Transgender Issues in Counseling,
www.algbtic.org

National Association of Social Workers (NASW), GLBT Issues,
www.socialworkers.org/diversity/new/glbt.asp

World Professional Association for Transgender Health (WPATH),
www.wpath.org (You can obtain a copy of the Standards of Care at this Web site.)

Youth-Specific Organizations
Camp Aranu'tiq,
(617) 467-5830,
www.camparanutiq.org

Gay, Lesbian and Straight Education Network (GLSEN),
(212) 727-0135,
www.glsen.org

Gender Odyssey Family,
www.genderodysseyfamily.org

Gender Spectrum,
(510) 567-3977,
www.genderspectrum.org

Trans Youth Equality Foundation,
(207) 478-4087,
www.transyouthequality.org

TransYouth Family Allies (TYFA),
(888) 462-8932,
www.imatyfa.org

Trevor Project,
(310) 271-8845 (office), (866) 488-7386 (suicide hotline),
www.thetrevorproject.org

YES Institute, (305) 663-7195, www.yesinstitute.org

Nationwide Support-Based Organizations
FTM International,
(877) 267-1440,
www.ftmi.org

Parents, Families and Friends of Lesbians and Gays (PFLAG),
(202) 467-8180,
www.pflag.org

Renaissance Transgender Association,
www.ren.org

TransFamily,
(216) 691-4357 (Emergency Resource Hotline),
www.transfamily.org

Transgender American Veterans Association,
www.tavausa.org

Literature Not Listed in the Bibliography but Worth Reading

Bohjalian, Chris. *Trans-Sister Radio*. New York: Vintage Books, 2000.

Bono, Chaz. *Transition: The Story of How I Became a Man*. New York: Dutton, 2011.

Ehrensaft, Diane. *Gender Born, Gender Made*. New York: The Experiment, 2011.

Feinberg, Leslie. *Stone Butch Blues*. New York: Alyson Books, 1993.

Green, Jamison. *Becoming a Visible Man*. Nashville: Vanderbilt University Press, 2004.

Herman, Joanne. *Transgender Explained for Those Who Are Not*. Bloomington, IN: AuthorHouse, 2009.

Kailey, Matt. *Just Add Hormones*. Boston: Beacon, 2005.

Mallon, Gerald P., ed. *Social Work Practice with Transgender and Gender Variant Youth*. New York: Routledge, 2009.

Outreach Program for Children with Gender-Variant Behaviors and Their Families "If You Are Concerned about Your Child's Gender Behaviors." Washington, DC: Children's National Medical Center, 2003, http://www.dcchildrens.com/dcchildrens/about/pdf/GenVar.pdf.

PFLAG Transgender Network. *Our Trans Children*. Washington, DC: PFLAG, 2007, http://community.pflag.org.

Stryker, Susan, and Stephen Whittle, eds. *The Transgender Studies Reader*. New York: Routledge, 2006.

NOTES

1. WHAT DOES IT MEAN TO BE TRANSGENDER?

1. I first did this exercise during an educational training at the YES Institute in Miami, Florida, in January 2009. See http://www.yesinstitute.org.
2. "Sex," Def. 1, Merriam-Webster Online Dictionary, 2009, http://www.merriam-webster.com/dictionary/sex.
3. "Gender," Def. 2b, Merriam-Webster Online Dictionary, 2009, http://www.merriam-webster.com/dictionary/gender.
4. "Binary," Merriam-Webster Online Dictionary, 2009, http://www.merriam-webster.com/dictionary/binary.
5. "Terminology," University of Minnesota Transgender Commission, March 11, 2008, http://glbta.umn.edu/trans/terms.html.
6. World Professional Association of Transgender Health, *The Standards of Care for Gender Identity Disorders*, 6th version (Minneapolis: WPATH, 2005).
7. Human Rights Campaign, "Transgender Population and Number of Transgender Employees," 2009, http://www.hrc.org/issues/9598.htm.

2. SEXUAL ORIENTATION VERSUS GENDER

1. Kinsey Institute, "Kinsey's Heterosexual-Homosexual Rating Scale," revised 2009, http://www.kinseyinstitute.org/resources/ak-hhscale.html.
2. Alfred Kinsey, Wardell R. Pomeroy, and Clyde E. Martin, *Sexual Behavior in the Human Male* (Philadelphia: Saunders, 1948); Alfred Kinsey, Wardell R. Pomeroy, Clyde E. Martin, and P. Gebhard, *Sexual Behavior in the Human Female* (Philadelphia: Saunders, 1953).
3. Annamarie Jagose and Don Kulick, "Thinking Sex/Thinking Gender," *GLQ: A Journal of Lesbian and Gay Studies* 10, no. 2 (2004): 211.
4. Pagan Kennedy, *The First Man-Made Man* (New York: Bloomsbury, 2008).
5. Judith Halberstam, "Transgender Butch: Butch/FTM Border Wars and the Masculine Continuum," *GLQ: A Journal of Lesbian and Gay Studies* 4, no. 2 (1998): 287–310.
6. Angela Pattatucci Aragón, "Introduction: Challenging Lesbian Normativity," in Angela Pattatucci Aragón, ed., *Challenging Lesbian Norms*, pp. 8–10 (Binghamton, NY: Harrington Park).
7. Associated Press, "No Charges in Uncertain-Gender Wedding," June 30, 2008.

3. COMING OUT AS TRANSGENDER

1. Deana F. Morrow, "Gay, Lesbian, Bisexual, and Transgender Adolescents," in Deana F. Morrow and Lori Messenger, eds., *Sexual Orientation and Gender Expression in Social Work Practice*, 184 (New York: Columbia University Press, 2006).
2. Arlene Istar Lev, *Transgender Emergence* (Binghamton, NY: Haworth Clinical Practice), 243.
3. José B. Ashford, Craig Winston LeCroy, and Kathy L. Lortie, *Human Behavior in the Social Environment* (Belmont, CA: Thomson Brooks/Cole, 2006), 304–305.
4. Jennifer Finney Boylan, *She's Not There: A Life in Two Genders* (New York: Broadway Books, 2003), 216–217.
5. Jennifer Finney Boylan, "'Maddy' Just Might Work After All," *New York Times*, April 26, 2009.
6. Lev, *Transgender Emergence*, 312.
7. Mildred L. Brown and Chloe Ann Rounsley, *True Selves* (San Francisco: Jossey-Bass, 1996), 148.
8. Ibid., 150.

9. Stephanie G., *The Agony of Nurturing the Spirit* (Philadelphia: Parents, Family, and Friends of Lesbians and Gays of Philadelphia, 2006), 3–5.
10. Stephanie Brill and Rachel Pepper, *The Transgender Child* (San Francisco: Cleis, 2008), 61–62.
11. Ibid., 12.
12. Venessia Romero and Joseph Romero, personal interview, September 14, 2009.

4. TRANSITION

1. Autumn Sandeen, personal interview, July 9, 2009.
2. Matt Kailey, personal interview, September 26, 2009.
3. Louis J. Gooren and Henriette A. Delemarre-van de Waal, "Hormone Treatment of Adult and Juvenile Transsexual Patients," in Randi Ettner, Stan Monstrey, and A. Evan Eyler, eds., *Principles of Transgender Medicine and Surgery* (Binghamton, NY: Haworth, 2007), 77.
4. Ibid.
5. Marshall Dahl, Jamie L. Feldman, Joshua M. Goldberg, and Afshin Jaberi, "Physical Aspects of Transgender Endocrine Therapy," *International Journal of Transgenderism* 9, no. 3/4 (2006): 114.
6. Ibid., 113.
7. A. Evan Eyler, "Primary Medical Care of the Gender-Variant Patient," in Randi Ettner, Stan Monstrey, and A. Evan Eyler, eds., *Principles of Transgender Medicine and Surgery* (Binghamton, NY: Haworth, 2007), 26.
8. Dahl et al., "Physical Aspects of Transgender Endocrine Therapy," 114.
9. Ibid., 118.
10. Gooren and Delemarre-van de Waal, "Hormone Treatment of Adult and Juvenile Transsexual Patients," 79.
11. Arlene Istar Lev, *Transgender Emergence* (Binghamton, NY: Haworth Clinical Practice, 2004), 262.
12. University of Michigan Health System, "Binding FAQ," 2009, http://www.med.umich.edu/transgender/Binding%20FAQ.pdf.
13. Gooren and Delemarre-van de Waal, "Hormone Treatment of Adult and Juvenile Transsexual Patients," 80.
14. Dahl et al., "Physical Aspects of Transgender Endocrine Therapy," 118.
15. Ibid.
16. Stan Monstrey, Gennaro Selvaggi, and Peter Ceulemans, "Surgery: Male-to-Female Patient," in Randi Ettner, Stan Monstrey, and A. Evan Eyler, eds., *Principles of Transgender Medicine and Surgery* (Binghamton, NY: Haworth, 2007), 120–122.

17. Gary Alter, "Penile Skin Inversion Technique," 2004, http://www.altermd.com/Transsexual%20Surgery/male_to_female.htm.
18. Monstrey et al., "Surgery: Male-to-Female Patient," 112–113.
19. Marci Bowers, "MTF: Trachea Shave," 2010, http://www.marcibowers.com/grs/tracheal.html.
20. Stan Monstrey, Peter Ceulemans, and Peter Hoebeke, "Surgery: Female-to-Male Patient," in Randi Ettner, Stan Monstrey, and A. Evan Eyler, eds., *Principles of Transgender Medicine and Surgery* (Binghamton, NY: Haworth, 2007), 153.
21. Ibid., 150.
22. Ibid.
23. Ibid., 153.
24. World Professional Association for Transgender Health, *The Standards of Care for Gender Identity Disorders*, 6th version (Minneapolis: WPATH, 2005).
25. World Professional Association for Transgender Health, "Criteria for Hormone Therapy," in *The Standards of Care for the Health of Transsexual, Transgender, and Gender Nonconforming People*, 7th version (Minneapolis: WPATH, 2011), 34.
26. Ibid., 58–60.
27. Ibid.
28. Ibid., 26.
29. Ibid., 27–28.
30. Ibid., 28–29.
31. U.S. Department of State, "New Policy on Gender Change in Passports Announced," June 9, 2010, http://www.state.gov/r/pa/prs/ps/2010/06/142922.htm.
32. TransYouth Family Allies, "Puberty Inhibitors, Reviewed by Dr. Norman P. Spack, M.D.," June 8, 2009.
33. Ibid.

5. THE HISTORY OF TRANSGENDERISM AND ITS EVOLUTION OVER TIME

1. Richard Ekins, "Science, Politics and Clinical Intervention: Harry Benjamin, Transsexualism and the Problem of Heteronormativity," *Sexualities* 8, no. 3 (2005): 306.
2. Darryl B. Hill, "Dear Doctor Benjamin: Letters from Transsexual Youth (1963–1976)," *International Journal of Transgenderism* 10, no. 3/4 (2008): 150.

3. Leah Cahan Schaefer and Connie Christine Wheeler, "Harry Benjamin's First Ten Cases (1938–1953): A Clinical Historical Note," *Archives of Sexual Behavior* 24, no. 1 (1995): 73–93.
4. Arlene Istar Lev, *Transgender Emergence* (Binghamton, NY: Haworth Clinical Practice, 2004), 74.
5. Charles L. Ihlenfeld, "Harry Benjamin and Psychiatrists," in Ubaldo Leli and Jack Drescher, eds., *Transgender Subjectivities: A Clinician's Guide* (Binghamton, NY: Haworth Medical, 2004), 148.
6. Hill, "Dear Doctor Benjamin," 150.
7. Ibid., 169.
8. Ibid., 155.
9. Ihlenfeld, "Harry Benjamin and Psychiatrists," 150.
10. Christine Jorgensen, *Christine Jorgensen: A Personal Autobiography* (New York: Paul S. Eriksson, 1967), 79.
11. Ekins, "Science, Politics and Clinical Intervention," 150.
12. Jorgensen, *Christine Jorgensen*, 2.
13. Stan Monstrey, Gennaro Selvaggi, and Peter Ceulemans, "Surgery: Male-to-Female Patient," in Randi Ettner, Stan Monstrey, and A. Evan Eyler, eds., *Principles of Transgender Medicine and Surgery* (Binghamton, NY: Haworth, 2007), 107.
14. Patricia Gherovici, *Please Select Your Gender* (New York: Routledge, 2010), 221;
15. Associated Press, "Bronx 'Boy' Is Now a Girl," *New York Times*, December 2, 1952.
16. Joanne Meyerowitz, *How Sex Changed* (Cambridge: Harvard University Press, 2002), 212–213.
17. Ibid., 286.
18. Sanjida O'Connell, producer, *Dr. Money and the Boy with No Penis* (BBC Horizon, 2004).
19. John Colapinto, "Gender Gap: What Were the Real Reasons Behind David Reimer's Suicide?" *Slate*, June 3, 2004.
20. O'Connell, *Dr. Money and the Boy with No Penis*.
21. Ibid.
22. John Colapinto, *As Nature Made Him: The Boy Who Was Raised as a Girl* (New York: Harper Collins, 2000), 56.
23. Ibid., 141.
24. O'Connell, *Dr. Money and the Boy with No Penis*.
25. Colapinto, *As Nature Made Him*, 205–210.
26. O'Connell, *Dr. Money and the Boy with No Penis*.
27. Colapinto, "Gender Gap," 4.
28. Susan Stryker, *Transgender History* (Berkeley, CA: Seal, 2008), 39.

29. Ibid., 79–80.
30. Meyerowitz, *How Sex Changed*, 149.
31. Stryker, *Transgender History*, 83–85.
32. Metropolitan Community Church of New York Homeless Youth Services, "Sylvia's Place," http://www.homelessyouthservices.org/placetostay.html.
33. David W. Dunlap, "Sylvia Rivera, 50, Figure in Birth of the Gay Liberation Movement," *New York Times*, February 20, 2002.
34. Stryker, *Transgender History*, 119.
35. FTM International, "FTM International Facts," 2010, http://www.ftmi.org.
36. Stryker, *Transgender History*, 120.
37. Joan Roughgarden, *Evolution's Rainbow* (Berkeley: University of California Press, 2004), 23.
38. Ibid., 27–28.
39. Ibid.
40. Peter Buston, "Size and Growth Modification in Clownfish," *Nature* 424 (2003): 145; Roughgarden, *Evolution's Rainbow*, 33.
41. Roughgarden, Evolution's Rainbow, 227.
42. Antony Thomas, *Middle Sexes: Redefining He and She* (HBO Films, 2005).
43. Michael G. Peletz, "Transgenderism and Gender Pluralism in Southeast Asia since Early Modern Times," *Current Anthropology* 47, no. 2 (2006): 312.
44. Sam Winter, "Thai Transgenders in Focus: Demographics, Transitions and Identities," *International Journal of Transgenderism* 9, no. 1 (2006): 17.
45. Pauline Park and John Manzon-Santos, "Issues of Transgendered Asian Americans and Pacific Islanders," Asian and Pacific Islander Wellness Center, 2000, http://www.apiwellness.org/article_tg_issues.html.
46. Sandeep Bakshi, "A Comparative Analysis of Hijras and Drag Queens: The Subversive Possibilities and Limits of Parading Effeminacy and Negotiating Masculinity," *Journal of Homosexuality* 46, no. 3/4 (2004): 214.
47. Leslie Feinberg, *Transgender Warriors* (Boston: Beacon, 1996), 44–45.
48. Ibid., 79.
49. Sabine Lang, *Men as Women, Women as Men: Changing Gender in Native American Cultures* (Austin: University of Texas Press, 1998), 113.
50. Katherine Walker, "Two-Spirited and Proud," *CBC News Viewpoint*, August 5, 2004.
51. NorthEast Two-Spirit Society, "Gender Roles of Two Spirit People," 2010, http://www.ne2ss.org/history.

52. Wesley Thomas, "Navajo Cultural Constructions of Gender and Sexuality," in Sue-Ellen Jacobs, Wesley Thomas, and Sabine Lang, eds., *Two-Spirit People* (Urbana: University of Illinois Press, 1997), 161–163.
53. Ibid.
54. Ibid., 165.
55. Carrie H. House, "Navajo Warrior Women," in Sue-Ellen Jacobs, Wesley Thomas, and Sabine Lang, eds., *Two-Spirit People* (Urbana: University of Illinois Press, 1997), 225.
56. Feinberg, *Transgender Warriors*, 106.
57. DeAnne Blanton, "Women Soldiers of the Civil War," *U.S. National Archives and Records Administration* 25, no. 1 (1993): 1–11.
58. National Park Service, U.S. Department of the Interior, "They Fought Like Men . . . Irish Women in the Civil War" (Vicksburg: National Park Service, n.d.).
59. Ibid.
60. Ibid.

6. TRANSGENDERISM AS A MENTAL HEALTH ISSUE

1. American Psychiatric Association, *Diagnostic and Statistical Manual of Mental Disorders*, 4th ed., text rev. (Arlington, VA: American Psychiatric Association, 2000).
2. American Psychiatric Association. "Gender Dysphoria." DSM-5 Development. 2011, http://www.dsm5.org/ProposedRevision/Pages/GenderDysphoria.aspx).
3. Arlene Istar Lev, *Transgender Emergence* (Binghamton, NY: Haworth Clinical Practice, 2004), 158.
4. American Psychiatric Association, *Diagnostic and Statistical Manual of Mental Disorders*, 4th ed., text rev., 581.
5. Ibid.
6. Intersex Society of North America, "What Is Intersex?" 2008, http://www.isna.org/faq/what_is_intersex.
7. American Psychiatric Association, *Diagnostic and Statistical Manual of Mental Disorders*, 4th ed., text rev., 581.
8. This diagnosis was in draft state when this book was published; therefore, it was speculated that these changes would occur in the 2013 publication of the *DSM-5*, but the changes could not be confirmed.
9. American Psychiatric Association. "Gender Dysphoria." DSM-5 Development. 2011, http://www.dsm5.org/ProposedRevision/Pages/GenderDysphoria.aspx.

10. Ibid.
11. Ibid.
12. Ibid.
13. Ibid.
14. Ibid.
15. Benjamin J. Sadock and Virginia A. Sadock, *Kaplan and Sadock's Synopsis of Psychiatry*, 10th ed. (Philadelphia: Lippincott Williams and Wilkins, 2007), 722.
16. Endocrine Society, "About Us," 2009, http://www.endo-society.org/about/index.cfm.
17. Wylie C. Hembree et al., "Endocrine Treatment of Transsexual Persons: An Endocrine Society Clinical Practice Guideline," *Journal of Clinical Endocrinology and Metabolism* 94, no. 9 (2009): 3137.
18. There are people who may have borderline personality disorder and GID simultaneously; the same goes for dissociative identity disorder or other mental illnesses as well. In this section, I only discuss those who are screened to make sure that they have GID and not a different condition.
19. Alix Spiegel, "Two Families Grapple with Sons' Gender Preferences," *All Things Considered*, National Public Radio, May 7, 2008.
20. Randall Ehrbar, Kelley Winters, and Nick Gorton, "Revision Suggestions for Gender Related Diagnoses in the DSM and ICD," presented at WPATH 2009 XXI Biennial Symposium, Oslo, Norway, June 19, 2009, http://www.gidreform.org/wpath2009EWG.html.
21. Kelley Winters, *Gender Madness in American Psychiatry* (Dillon, CO: GID Reform Advocates, 2008), 102.
22. Hembree et al., "Endocrine Treatment of Transsexual Persons."
23. Merriam-Webster Online Medical Dictionary, "Remission," 2009, http://www.merriam-webster.com/medical/remission.
24. Hembree et al., "Endocrine Treatment of Transsexual Persons."
25. American Medical Association House of Delegates, "Removing Financial Barriers to Care for Transgender Patients," April 18, 2008, http://www.ama-assn.org/ama1/pub/upload/mm/471/122.doc.
26. Agence France-Press, "La Transsexualité Ne Sera Plus Classée Comme Affectation Psychiatrique," *Le Monde Online*, May 16, 2009.
27. Stanley R. Vance Jr., et al., "Opinions about the DSM Gender Identity Disorder Diagnosis: Results from an International Survey Administered to Organizations Concerned with the Welfare of Transgender People," *International Journal of Transgenderism* 12, no. 1 (2010): 10.
28. American Psychological Association. "APA Policy Statement: Transgender, Gender Identity, and Gender Expression Non-Discrimination." August

2008, http://www.apa.org/about/governance/council/policy/transgender.aspx.

29. Winters, *Gender Madness in American Psychiatry*, 150–151.
30. American Psychiatric Association, *Diagnostic and Statistical Manual of Mental Disorders*, 4th ed., text rev., 578.
31. Ibid.

7. DISCRIMINATION

1. National Gay and Lesbian Task Force, "State Nondiscrimination Laws in the U.S.," 2009, http://www.thetaskforce.org/downloads/reports/issue_maps/non_discrimination_7_09_color.pdf.
2. Kendall Thomas, "Afterword: Are Transgender Rights Inhuman Rights?" in Paisley Currah, Richard M. Juang, and Shannon Price Minter, eds., *Transgender Rights* (Minneapolis: University of Minnesota Press, 2006), 315.
3. Ben Pershing, "Senate Passes Measure That Would Protect Gays," *Washington Post*, October 23, 2009.
4. Library of Congress, "H.R. 2017 CRS Summary," Bill Summary and Status, 111th Congress (2009–2010).
5. Jennifer L. Levi and Bennett H. Klein, "Pursuing Protection for Transgender People Through Disability Laws," in Paisley Currah, Richard M. Juang, and Shannon Price Minter, eds., *Transgender Rights* (Minneapolis: University of Minnesota Press, 2006), 80.
6. Shannon Minter, personal interview, October 6, 2010.
7. Dylan Forest, "A Boy in the Girls' Bathroom," in David Levithan and Billy Merrell, eds., *The Full Spectrum: A New Generation of Writing about Gay, Lesbian, Bisexual, Transgender Questioning, and Other Identities* (New York: Alfred A. Knopf, 2006), 123.
8. Sharon Ortiz, State of Washington Human Rights Commission, letter to Lisa Mottet, Esq., March 10, 2009.
9. Ralph Rosenberg, Iowa Civil Rights Commission, letter to Lisa Mottet, Esq., April 1, 2009.
10. Taylor Flynn, "Ties That [Don't] Bind: Transgender Family Law and the Unmaking of Families," in Paisley Currah, Richard M. Juang, and Shannon Price Minter, eds., *Transgender Rights* (Minneapolis: University of Minnesota Press, 2006), 32–33; Jamison Green, personal communication, November 27, 2010.
11. Emily A. Greytak, Joseph G. Kosciw, and Elizabeth M. Diaz, "Harsh Realities: The Experiences of Transgender Youth in Our Nation's Schools" (New York: Gay, Lesbian and Straight Education Network, 2009), 10–15.

12. United Church of Christ, "Affirming the Participation and Ministry of Transgender People Within the United Church of Christ and Supporting Their Civil and Human Rights," United Church of Christ Twenty-Fourth General Synod, July 15, 2003.
13. Rev. Dr. Cameron Partridge, personal interview, September 5, 2010.
14. U.S. Census Bureau, "History: 1790 Overview," http://www.census.gov/history/www/through_the_decades/overview/1790.html.
15. U.S. Census Bureau, "History: 1870," http://www.census.gov/history/www/through_the_decades/index_of_questions/1870_1.html.
16. U.S. Census Bureau, "History: 1890," http://www.census.gov/history/www/through_the_decades/index_of_questions/1870_1.html.
17. U.S. Citizenship and Immigration Services, "Asylum," September 3, 2009, http://www.uscis.gov.
18. Servicemembers Legal Defense Network, "Transgender Service Members," October 2008, http://www.sldn.org/page/-/Website/Fact%20Sheets/Transgender%20Service%20Members.pdf.
19. Denny Meyer, "LeAnna Bradley: 37 Years of Service," *Gay Military Signal*, September 2009.
20. LeAnna Bradley, personal interview, September 7, 2010.
21. Meyer, "LeAnna Bradley."

8. LESSER-KNOWN TYPES OF TRANSGENDERISM

1. This is from an exercise at YES Institute, 2009, http://www.yesinstitute.org.
2. Micah Domingo, personal interview, October 4, 2010.
3. Deborah Rudacille, *The Riddle of Gender* (New York: Anchor Books, 2006), 223–224.
4. Reid Vanderburgh, "Appropriate Therapeutic Care for Families with Pre-Pubescent Transgender/Gender-Dissonant Children," *Child and Adolescent Social Work Journal* 26, no. 2 (2009): 147.
5. Helen Boyd, *My Husband Betty* (New York: Thunder's Mouth, 2003).
6. Ibid., 22.
7. Virginia Erhardt, *Head over Heels: Wives Who Stay with Cross-Dressers and Transsexuals* (Binghamton, NY: Haworth, 2007), 25–28.
8. Ibid., 82.
9. Ibid., 1.
10. Boyd, *My Husband Betty*, 48.
11. Antonio Panormita, *Hermaphroditus* (Lanham, MD: Lexington Books, 2001), 17.

12. Tom Mazur, Melissa Colsman, and David E. Sandberg, "Intersex: Definition, Examples, Gender Stability, and the Case Against Merging with Transsexualism," in Randi Ettner, Stan Monstrey, and A. Evan Eyler, eds., *Principles of Transgender Medicine and Surgery* (Binghamton, NY: Haworth, 2007), 242.
13. Intersex Society of North America, "What Is Intersex?" 2008, http://www.isna.org/faq/what_is_intersex.
14. Children's Hospital Boston, "Gender Management Service (GeMS) Clinic: About Us," 2007, http://www.childrenshospital.org/clinicalservices/Site2280/mainpageS2280P4.html.
15. Peter A. Lee, Christopher P. Houk, S. Faisal Ahmed, and Ieuan A. Hughes, "Consensus Statement on Management of Intersex Disorders," *Pediatrics* 118, no. 2 (2006): e488.
16. Consortium on the Management of Disorders of Sex Development, *Handbook for Parents* (Rohnert Park, CA: Intersex Society of North America, 2006), 3.
17. Joan Roughgarden, *The Genial Gene: Deconstructing Darwinian Selfishness* (Berkeley: University of California Press, 2009), 106.
18. Harvey J. Makadon, Kenneth H. Mayer, Jennifer Potter, and Hilary Goldhammer, *Fenway Guide to Gay, Lesbian, Bisexual, and Transgender Health* (Philadelphia: American College of Physicians, 2008), 394.
19. Ibid., 404.
20. Raven Kaldera, "Do It on the Dotted Line," in Joan Nestle, Clare Howell, and Riki Wilchins, eds., *GenderQueer: Voices from Beyond the Sexual Binary* (Los Angeles: Alyson Books, 2002), 158.
21. All the Kings Men, "Experience the World of All the Kings Men!" 2010, http://www.atkm.com.
22. Daniel Harris, *Diary of a Drag Queen* (New York: Carroll and Graf, 2005), vii.
23. Christopher Hagberg, personal interview, October 6, 2010.
24. Ibid.

APPENDIX A: GLOSSARY

1. "Gender," Def. 2b, Merriam-Webster Online Dictionary, 2009, http://www.merriam-webster.com/dictionary/gender.
2. "Terminology," University of Minnesota Transgender Commission, March 11, 2008, http://glbta.umn.edu/trans/terms.html.
3. Ibid.

4. Stan Monstrey, Peter Ceulemans, and Peter Hoebeke, "Surgery: Female-to-Male Patient," in Randi Ettner, Stan Monstrey, and A. Evan Eyler, eds., *Principles of Transgender Medicine and Surgery* (Binghamton, NY: Haworth, 2007), 161–162.
5. "Paraphilia," Merriam-Webster Online Dictionary, 2010, http://www.merriam-webster.com/dictionary/paraphilia.
6. Monstrey et al., "Surgery: Female-to-Male Patient," 150.
7. Ibid.
8. Sam Winter, "Thai Transgenders in Focus: Demographics, Transitions and Identities," *International Journal of Transgenderism* 9, no. 1, (2006): 17.
9. "Sex," Def. 1, Merriam-Webster Online Dictionary, 2009, http://www.merriam-webster.com/dictionary/sex.
10. World Professional Association of Transgender Health, *The Standards of Care for Gender Identity Disorders*, 6th version (Minneapolis: WPATH, 2005).
11. Stan Monstrey, Gennaro Selvaggi, and Peter Ceulemans, "Surgery: Male-to-Female Patient," in Randi Ettner, Stan Monstrey, and A. Evan Eyler, eds., *Principles of Transgender Medicine and Surgery* (Binghamton, NY: Haworth, 2007), 120–122.

BIBLIOGRAPHY

Agence France-Press. "La Transsexualité Ne Sera Plus Classée Comme Affectation Psychiatrique." *Le Monde Online*, May 16, 2009.

All the Kings Men, "Experience the World of All the Kings Men!" 2010, http://www.atkm.com.

Alter, Gary. "Penile Skin Inversion Technique." 2004, http://www.altermd.com/Transsexual%20Surgery/male_to_female.htm.

American Medical Association House of Delegates. "Removing Financial Barriers to Care for Transgender Patients." April 18, 2008, http://www.ama-assn.org/ama1/pub/upload/mm/471/122.doc.

American Psychiatric Association. *Diagnostic and Statistical Manual of Mental Disorders*, 4th ed., text rev. Arlington, VA: American Psychiatric Association, 2000.

American Psychiatric Association. "Proposed Revision—Gender Identity Disorder in Adolescents or Adults." *DSM-5 Development*. 2010, http://www.dsm5.org/ProposedRevisions/Pages/proposedrevision.aspx?rid=482.

American Psychiatric Association. "Gender Dysphoria." DSM-5 Development. 2011, http://www.dsm5.org/ProposedRevision/Pages/GenderDysphoria.aspx.

American Psychological Association. "APA Policy Statement: Transgender, Gender Identity, and Gender Expression Non-Discrimination." August 2008, http://www.apa.org/about/governance/council/policy/transgender.aspx.

Aragón, Angela Pattatucci. "Introduction: Challenging Lesbian Normativity." In Angela Pattatucci Aragón, ed., *Challenging Lesbian Norms*. Binghamton, NY: Harrington Park, 2006.

Ashford, José B., Craig Winston LeCroy, and Kathy L. Lortie. *Human Behavior in the Social Environment*. Belmont, CA: Thomson Brooks/Cole, 2006.

Associated Press. "Bronx 'Boy' Is Now a Girl." *New York Times,* December 2, 1952.

Associated Press. "No Charges in Uncertain-Gender Wedding." June 30, 2008.

Bakshi, Sandeep. "A Comparative Analysis of Hijras and Drag Queens: The Subversive Possibilities and Limits of Parading Effeminacy and Negotiating Masculinity." *Journal of Homosexuality* 46, no. 3/4 (February 2004): 211–223.

Blanton, DeAnne. "Women Soldiers of the Civil War." *U.S. National Archives and Records Administration* 25, no. 1 (Spring 1993): 1–11.

Bowers, Marci. "MTF: Trachea Shave." 2010, http://www.marcibowers.com/grs/tracheal.html.

Boyd, Helen. *My Husband Betty.* New York: Thunder's Mouth, 2003.

Boylan, Jennifer Finney. "'Maddy' Just Might Work after All." *New York Times,* April 26, 2009.

Boylan, Jennifer Finney. *She's Not There: A Life in Two Genders.* New York: Broadway Books, 2003.

Brill, Stephanie, and Rachel Pepper. *The Transgender Child.* San Francisco: Cleis, 2008.

Brown, Mildred L., and Chloe Ann Rounsley. *True Selves.* San Francisco: Jossey-Bass, 1996.

Buston, Peter. "Size and Growth Modification in Clownfish." *Nature* 424 (July 2003): 145–146.

Children's Hospital Boston. "Gender Management Service (GeMS) Clinic: About Us." 2007, http://www.childrenshospital.org/clinicalservices/Site2280/mainpageS2280P4.html.

Colapinto, John. *As Nature Made Him: The Boy Who Was Raised as a Girl.* New York: Harper Collins, 2000.

Colapinto, John. "Gender Gap: What Were the Real Reasons Behind David Reimer's Suicide?" *Slate,* June 3, 2004, http://www.slate.com/id/2101678.

Consortium on the Management of Disorders of Sex Development. *Handbook for Parents.* Rohnert Park, CA: Intersex Society of North America, 2006.

Dahl, Marshall, Jamie L. Feldman, Joshua M. Goldberg, and Afshin Jaberi. "Physical Aspects of Transgender Endocrine Therapy." *International Journal of Transgenderism* 9, no. 3–4 (July 2006): 111–134.

Dunlap, David W. "Sylvia Rivera, 50, Figure in Birth of the Gay Liberation Movement." *New York Times*, February 20, 2002.

Ehrbar, Randall, Kelley Winters, and Nick Gorton. "Revision Suggestions for Gender Related Diagnoses in the DSM and ICD." Presented at WPATH 2009 XXI Biennial Symposium. Oslo, Norway, June 19, 2009, http://www.gidreform.org/wpath2009EWG.html.

Ekins, Richard. "Science, Politics and Clinical Intervention: Harry Benjamin, Transsexualism and the Problem of Heteronormativity." *Sexualities* 8, no. 3 (July 2005): 306–328.

Endocrine Society. "About Us." 2009, http://www.endo-society.org/about/index.cfm.

Erhardt, Virginia. *Head over Heels: Wives Who Stay with Cross-Dressers and Transsexuals*. Binghamton, NY: Haworth, 2007.

Eyler, A. Evan. "Primary Medical Care of the Gender-Variant Patient." In Randi Ettner, Stan Monstrey, and A. Evan Eyler, eds., *Principles of Transgender Medicine and Surgery*. Binghamton, NY: Haworth, 2007.

Faderman, Lillian, Horacio Roque Ramirez, Yolanda Retter, Stuart Timmons, and Eric C. Wat, eds. *Great Events from History: Gay, Lesbian, Bisexual, Transgender Events, Vol. I: 1848–1983; Vol. II: 1984–2006*. Pasadena, CA: Salem, 2007.

Feinberg, Leslie. *Transgender Warriors*. Boston: Beacon, 1996.

Flynn, Taylor. "Ties That [Don't] Bind: Transgender Family Law and the Unmaking of Families." In Paisley Currah, Richard M. Juang, and Shannon Price Minter, eds., *Transgender Rights*. Minneapolis: University of Minnesota Press, 2006.

Forest, Dylan. "A Boy in the Girls' Bathroom." In David Levithan and Billy Merrell, eds., *The Full Spectrum: A New Generation of Writing about Gay, Lesbian, Bisexual, Transgender Questioning, and Other Identities*. New York: Alfred A. Knopf, 2006.

FTM International. "FTM International Facts." 2010, http://www.ftmi.org.

G., Stephanie. *The Agony of Nurturing the Spirit*. Philadelphia: Parents, Family, and Friends of Lesbians and Gays of Philadelphia, 2006.

Gherovici, Patricia. *Please Select Your Gender*. New York: Routledge, 2010.

Gooren, Louis J. and Henriette A. Delemarre-van de Waal. "Hormone Treatment of Adult and Juvenile Transsexual Patients." In Randi Ettner, Stan Monstrey, and A. Evan Eyler, eds., *Principles of Transgender Medicine and Surgery*. Binghamton, NY: Haworth, 2007.

Greytak, Emily A., Joseph G. Kosciw, and Elizabeth M. Diaz. "Harsh Realities: The Experiences of Transgender Youth in Our Nation's Schools." New York: Gay, Lesbian and Straight Education Network, 2009.

Halberstam, Judith. "Transgender Butch: Butch/FTM Border Wars and the Masculine Continuum." *GLQ: A Journal of Lesbian and Gay Studies* 4, no. 2 (April 1998): 287–310.

Harris, Daniel. *Diary of a Drag Queen*. New York: Carroll and Graf, 2005.

Hembree, Wylie C., Peggy Cohen-Kettenis, Henriette A. Delemarre-van de Waal, Louis J. Gooren, Walter J. Meyer III, Norman P. Spack, Vin Tangpricha, and Victor M. Montori. "Endocrine Treatment of Transsexual Persons: An Endocrine Society Clinical Practice Guideline." *Journal of Clinical Endocrinology and Metabolism* 94, no. 9 (September 2009): 3132–3154.

Hill, Darryl B. "Dear Doctor Benjamin: Letters from Transsexual Youth (1963–1976)." *International Journal of Transgenderism* 10, no. 3–4 (December 2008): 149–170.

House, Carrie H. "Navajo Warrior Women." In Sue-Ellen Jacobs, Wesley Thomas, and Sabine Lang, eds., *Two-Spirit People*. Urbana: University of Illinois Press, 1997.

Human Rights Campaign. "Transgender Population and Number of Transgender Employees." 2009, http://www.hrc.org/issues/9598.htm.

Ihlenfeld, Charles L. "Harry Benjamin and Psychiatrists." In Ubaldo Leli and Jack Drescher, eds., *Transgender Subjectivities: A Clinician's Guide*. Binghamton, NY: Haworth Medical, 2004.

Intersex Society of North America. "What Is Intersex?" 2008, http://www.isna.org/faq/what_is_intersex.

Jagose, Annamarie and Don Kulick. "Thinking Sex/Thinking Gender." *GLQ: A Journal of Lesbian and Gay Studies* 10, no. 2 (April 2004): 211–312.

Jorgensen, Christine. *Christine Jorgensen: A Personal Autobiography*. New York: Paul S. Eriksson, 1967.

Kaldera, Raven. "Do It on the Dotted Line." In Joan Nestle, Clare Howell, and Riki Wilchins, eds., *GenderQueer: Voices from Beyond the Sexual Binary*. Los Angeles: Alyson Books, 2002.

Kennedy, Pagan. *The First Man-Made Man*. New York: Bloomsbury, 2008.

Kinsey, Alfred, Wardell R. Pomeroy, and Clyde E. Martin. *Sexual Behavior in the Human Male*. Philadelphia: Saunders, 1948.

Kinsey, Alfred, Wardell R. Pomeroy, Clyde E. Martin, and P. Gebhard. *Sexual Behavior in the Human Female*. Philadelphia: Saunders, 1953.

Kinsey Institute. "Kinsey's Heterosexual-Homosexual Rating Scale," revised 2009, http://www.kinseyinstitute.org/resources/ak-hhscale.html.

Lang, Sabine. *Men as Women, Women as Men: Changing Gender in Native American Cultures*. Austin: University of Texas Press, 1998.

Lee, Peter A., Christopher P. Houk, S. Faisal Ahmed, and Ieuan A. Hughes. "Consensus Statement on Management of Intersex Disorders." *Pediatrics* 118, no. 2 (August 2006): e488–e500.

Lev, Arlene Istar. *Transgender Emergence*. Binghamton, NY: Haworth Clinical Practice, 2004.

Levi, Jennifer L. and Bennett H. Klein. "Pursuing Protection for Transgender People Through Disability Laws." In Paisley Currah, Richard M. Juang, and Shannon Price Minter, eds., *Transgender Rights*. Minneapolis: University of Minnesota Press, 2006.

Library of Congress. "H.R. 2017 CRS Summary." Bill Summary and Status 111th Congress (2009–2010).

Makadon, Harvey J., Kenneth H. Mayer, Jennifer Potter, and Hilary Goldhammer. *Fenway Guide to Gay, Lesbian, Bisexual, and Transgender Health*. Philadelphia: American College of Physicians, 2008.

Mazur, Tom, Melissa Colsman, and David E. Sandberg. "Intersex: Definition, Examples, Gender Stability, and the Case Against Merging with Transsexualism." In Randi Ettner, Stan Monstrey, and A. Evan Eyler, eds., *Principles of Transgender Medicine and Surgery*. Binghamton, NY: Haworth, 2007.

Merriam-Webster Online Dictionary. "Binary." http://www.merriam-webster.com/dictionary/binary.

Merriam-Webster Online Dictionary. "Gender; def 2b." http://www.merriam-webster.com/dictionary/gender.

Merriam-Webster Online Dictionary "Sex; def 1." http://www.merriam-webster.com/dictionary/sex.

Metropolitan Community Church of New York Homeless Youth Services. "Sylvia's Place." http://www.homelessyouthservices.org/placetostay.html.

Meyer, Denny. "LeAnna Bradley: 37 Years of Service." *Gay Military Signal*, September 2009.

Meyerowitz, Joanne. *How Sex Changed*. Cambridge: Harvard University Press, 2002.

Minnesota Department of Human Rights. "When Gender and Gender Identity Are Not the Same." *The Rights Stuff*, November 2006, http://www.humanrights.state.mn.us/education/articles/rs06_4gender_protections.html.

Monstrey, Stan, Peter Ceulemans, and Peter Hoebeke. "Surgery: Female-to-Male Patient." In Randi Ettner, Stan Monstrey, and A. Evan Eyler, eds., *Principles of Transgender Medicine and Surgery*. Binghamton, NY: Haworth, 2007.

Monstrey, Stan, Gennaro Selvaggi, and Peter Ceulemans. "Surgery: Male-to-Female Patient." In Randi Ettner, Stan Monstrey, and A. Evan Eyler, eds., *Principles of Transgender Medicine and Surgery*. Binghamton, NY: Haworth Press, 2007.

Morrow, Deana F. "Gay, Lesbian, Bisexual, and Transgender Adolescents." In Deana F. Morrow and Lori Messenger, eds., *Sexual Orientation and Gender Expression in Social Work Practice*. New York: Columbia University Press, 2006.

National Gay and Lesbian Task Force. "State Nondiscrimination Laws in the U.S." 2009, http://www.thetaskforce.org/downloads/reports/issue_maps/non_discrimination_7_09_color.pdf.

National Park Service, U.S. Department of the Interior. "They Fought Like Men . . . Irish Women in the Civil War." Vicksburg: National Park Service, n.d.

NorthEast Two-Spirit Society. "Gender Roles of Two Spirit People." 2010, http://www.ne2ss.org/history.

O'Connell, Sanjida, producer. *Dr. Money and the Boy with No Penis.* BBC Horizon, 2004.

Panormita, Antonio. *Hermaphroditus*. Lanham, MD: Lexington Books, 2001.

Park, Pauline and John Manzon-Santos. "Issues of Transgendered Asian Americans and Pacific Islanders." Asian and Pacific Islander Wellness Center. October 2000, http://www.apiwellness.org/article_tg_issues.html.

Peletz, Michael G. "Transgenderism and Gender Pluralism in Southeast Asia since Early Modern Times." *Current Anthropology* 47, no. 2 (April 2006): 309–340.

Pershing, Ben. "Senate Passes Measure That Would Protect Gays." *Washington Post*, October 23, 2009.

Roughgarden, Joan. *Evolution's Rainbow*. Berkeley: University of California Press, 2004.

Roughgarden, Joan. *The Genial Gene: Deconstructing Darwinian Selfishness*. Berkeley: University of California Press, 2009.

Rudacille, Deborah. *The Riddle of Gender*. New York: Anchor Books, 2006.

Sadock, Benjamin J. and Virginia A. Sadock. *Kaplan and Sadock's Synopsis of Psychiatry*, 10th ed. Philadelphia: Lippincott Williams and Wilkins, 2007.

Schaefer, Leah Cahan and Connie Christine Wheeler. "Harry Benjamin's First Ten Cases (1938–1953): A Clinical Historical Note." *Archives of Sexual Behavior* 24, no. 1 (February 1995): 73–93.

Servicemembers Legal Defense Network. "Transgender Service Members." October 2008, http://www.sldn.org/page/-/Website/Fact%20Sheets/Transgender%20Service%20Members.pdf.

Spiegel, Alix. "Two Families Grapple with Sons' Gender Preferences." *All Things Considered,* National Public Radio, May 7, 2008.

Stryker, Susan. "Dr. Harry Benjamin (1885–1986)." GLBTQ: An Encyclopedia of Gay, Lesbian, Bisexual, Transgender, and Queer Culture, http://www.glbtq.com/social-sciences/benjamin_h.html.

Stryker, Susan. *Transgender History*. Berkeley, CA: Seal, 2008.

Thomas, Antony. *Middle Sexes: Redefining He and She*. HBO Films, 2005.

Thomas, Kendall. "Afterword: Are Transgender Rights Inhuman Rights?" In Paisley Currah, Richard M. Juang, and Shannon Price Minter, eds., *Transgender Rights*. Minneapolis: University of Minnesota Press, 2006.

Thomas, Wesley. "Navajo Cultural Constructions of Gender and Sexuality." In Sue-Ellen Jacobs, Wesley Thomas, and Sabine Lang, eds., *Two-Spirit People*. Urbana: University of Illinois Press, 1997.

Transgender Law and Policy Institute and the National Gay and Lesbian Task Force. 2006. "Scope of Explicitly Transgender-Inclusive Anti-Discrimination Laws." http://www.transgenderlaw.org/ndlaws/ngltftlpichart.pdf.

TransYouth Family Allies. "Puberty Inhibitors." June 8, 2009, http://www.imatyfa.org/permanent_files/pubertyblockers101.html.

United Church of Christ. "Affirming the Participation and Ministry of Transgender People Within the United Church of Christ and Supporting Their Civil and Human Rights." United Church of Christ Twenty-Fourth General Synod, July 15, 2003, http://www.ucccoalition.org/programs/ona/background/2003_general_synod_transgender_people/.

University of Michigan Health System. "Binding FAQ." 2009, http://www.med.umich.edu/transgender/Binding%20FAQ.pdf.

University of Minnesota Transgender Commission. "Terminology." 2008, http://glbta.umn.edu/trans/terms.html.

U.S. Census Bureau. "History: 1790 Overview." http://www.census.gov/history/www/through_the_decades/overview/1790.html.

U.S. Census Bureau. "History: 1870." http://www.census.gov/history/www/through_the_decades/index_of_questions/1870_1.html.

U.S. Census Bureau. "History: 1890." http://www.census.gov/history/www/through_the_decades/index_of_questions/1890_1.html.

U.S. Citizenship and Immigration Services. "Asylum." September 3, 2009, http://www.uscis.gov.

U.S. Department of State. "New Policy on Gender Change in Passports Announced." June 9, 2010, http://www.state.gov/r/pa/prs/ps/2010/06/142922.htm.

Vance, Stanley R., Jr., Peggy T. Cohen-Kettenis, Jack Drescher, Heino F. L. Meyer-Bahlburg, Friedemann Pfäfflin, and Kenneth J. Zucker. "Opinions about the *DSM* Gender Identity Disorder Diagnosis: Results from an International Survey Administered to Organizations Concerned with the Welfare of Transgender People." *International Journal of Transgenderism* 12, no. 1 (January–March 2010): 1–14.

Vanderburgh, Reid. "Appropriate Therapeutic Care for Families with Pre-Pubescent Transgender/Gender-Dissonant Children." *Child and Adolescent Social Work Journal* 26, no. 2 (April 2009): 135–154.

Walker, Katherine. "Two-Spirited and Proud." *CBC News Viewpoint*, August 5, 2004.

Winter, Sam. "Thai Transgenders in Focus: Demographics, Transitions and Identities." *International Journal of Transgenderism* 9, no. 1 (April 2006): 15–27.

Winters, Kelley. *Gender Madness in American Psychiatry*. Dillon, CO: GID Reform Advocates, 2008.
World Professional Association for Transgender Health. *The Standards of Care for Gender Identity Disorders*, 6th version. Minneapolis: WPATH, 2005.
World Professional Association for Transgender Health. *The Standards of Care for the Health of Transsexual, Transgender, and Gender Nonconforming People*, 7th version. Minneapolis: WPATH, 2011.

INDEX